THE BATTLE OF
WATERLOO

EUROPE IN THE BALANCE

THE BATTLE OF
WATERLOO

EUROPE IN THE BALANCE

ARCTURUS

ARCTURUS
This edition published in 2016 by Arcturus Publishing Limited
26/27 Bickels Yard, 151–153 Bermondsey Street,
London SE1 3HA

Typesetting by Palimpsest Book Production Limited
Cover image: courtesy of The National Army Museum/Mary Evans
Picture Library

ISBN: 978-1-78599-020-5
DA004651UK

Printed in China

CONTENTS

INTRODUCTION

'THEY HAVE LEARNED NOTHING AND FORGOTTEN NOTHING'

Charles Talleyrand, on the situation in France in 1814 under Louis XVIII

The battle fought on 18 June 1815 just to the south of Waterloo in what is now Belgium proved to be the decisive engagement in the final campaign of a war that had torn Europe apart for 23 years. Fighting had spread around the world as the combatant states sought to gain advantages that eluded them in Europe. The death toll of these long years of war will never be properly known. Certainly, millions died as a direct result of the fighting and millions more in the famines and epidemics that followed the armies and the disruptions they caused. Economically, Europe was left prostrate – with hardship and unemployment making worse the misery of the wars themselves.

Revolutionary fervour
The conflict had been sparked by the French Revolution, which began in 1789. When the Revolution first erupted, it had been seen very much as an internal French matter. The government of King Louis XVI was notoriously corrupt and inefficient, while the social injustices of the regime were well known. Many people across Europe – even some monarchs – welcomed the early stages of the Revolution, seeing it as a necessary reform of a hopeless system that might bring stability to a tottering regime.

However, the increasingly violent nature of the Revolution and sweeping claims of universal rights and freedoms made by the more extreme revolutionaries soon began to concern the more autocratic monarchs of Europe. In August 1791 Frederick William II of Prussia and Leopold of Austria issued the Pillnitz Declaration. This vaguely worded statement was intended to reaffirm the theoretical basis of monarchical power – partly to give some diplomatic aid to Louis, but mostly to give warning to reformers in the rulers' own realms that while reform might be possible, revolution was not. Unfortunately, the French government interpreted the declaration as a warning that Prussia and Austria were going to use military force to restore the dictatorial rule of Louis in France. Deciding to get their retaliation in first, France declared war on Austria in April 1792. Prussia rushed to aid Austria, while the Kingdom of Piedmont in northern Italy joined in, hoping to grab disputed border territories.

The early campaigns ended in stalemate. The French government became more extreme, abolishing the monarchy and executing Louis XVI. Revolutionary ideas spread rapidly across Europe, as peoples sought to throw off the shackles of serfdom and enjoy previously unheard-of freedoms – such as not going to church every Sunday, having a trial before being thrown in prison or being free to set up a business without having to pay a government official for permission. Some monarchs responded by encouraging reforms, others with repression – but the French invariably welcomed and encouraged such revolutionary movements. Europe was caught in an upheaval of social, legal and cultural turmoil every bit as disruptive as the wars that would engulf the continent.

Napoleon's rise and fall
Out of this turmoil emerged a single dominating figure: Napoleon Bonaparte. Born in 1769 into a family of minor Corsican nobility,

Opposite: Napoleon had himself crowned emperor in 1804. He retained the Revolution's social, legal and cultural features, but re-imposed the old monarchy's autocratic rule under his own control.

Napoleon joined the French army and enthusiastically embraced the principles of the Revolution. By a combination of military genius and political cunning, Napoleon made himself dictator of France by 1799 and in 1804 had himself crowned Emperor of the French. He instituted a composite regime that retained many of the social, legal and cultural features of the Revolution while reimposing the autocratic rule of the monarchy under his own control.

This potent mix of idealism and pragmatism emboldened revolutionaries outside France, and Napoleon himself. By 1807 Napoleon was master of Europe, heading a patchwork of regimes ruled by his relatives and cronies or by older dynasties cowed into subservience. Only Britain stood aside from French domination – safe beyond the English Channel, guarded by the ships of the Royal Navy.

In 1812, Napoleon accused Tsar Alexander I of Russia of plotting an alliance with Britain – and invaded. The 1812 campaign turned into a disaster for Napoleon as Russian resistance combined with savage winter weather to reduce Napoleon's army from 450,000 men to just 40,000.

Sensing French weakness, other European monarchs rose against Napoleon. Even reformists who welcomed revolutionary policies had come to resent French control and Napoleon's rapacious demands. A general coalition was formed against Napoleon. Wanting to avoid the horrors of more fighting, the coalition offered Napoleon peace if France returned to its pre-war boundaries. He refused – and by 1814 had been crushed.

Banished to Elba

On 4 April 1814 Napoleon abdicated the imperial throne of France. The allies gave him the small Mediterranean island of Elba to rule and allowed him a personal guard of 1,000 men. The French monarchy was reinstated in the shape of King Louis XVIII, younger brother of the executed Louis XVI. The allies had made Louis promise to accept most of the reforms of the Revolution as a price of restoration to his crown, but as soon as he was in power Louis ignored his promises.

Louis ensured that leading politicians of the Revolution and Empire were sacked, along with large numbers of government officials. He reintroduced old pre-Revolutionary laws and raised taxes. Louis announced a new democratic constitution, but then restricted the vote to just 90,000 wealthy men out of a population of more than 30 million.

Many French people feared not only that the bad days of corrupt and inefficient royalist government were coming back, but also that Louis was determined to pay off scores and settle the feuds of the Revolution. 'They have learned nothing and forgotten nothing,' quipped Napoleon's foreign minister Charles Talleyrand.

Trouble was brewing. And Napoleon was watching carefully from Elba.

CHAPTER 1

'THE MONSTER IS LOOSE'

French newspaper Le Moniteur **on Napoleon's escape from Elba, March 1815**

When he arrived on Elba in May 1814, Napoleon was uncertain what to do. He attempted suicide, but failed because he took ineffective poison. After this his spirits were restored by the arrival of a number of old adherents, admirers and friends.

In the months that followed, Napoleon threw himself into reforming the government and economy of the island. He put a lot of effort into improving the mines and into making agricultural output more profitable. These often long-term plans were aimed at increasing government revenue, on which Napoleon relied. The British Resident put on Elba to keep an eye on Napoleon, Sir Neil Campbell, became convinced that Napoleon was resigned to a life as a minor monarch and became a less frequent visitor to Napoleon's court.

In the opening weeks of 1815 a messenger was intercepted carrying letters between Napoleon and his one-time supporter Joachim Murat, King of Naples. This was a breach of the peace treaty, which forbade Napoleon to communicate with other rulers without permission. However, Murat was an old friend and, apparently, a firm Austrian ally so no real action was taken.

In fact, Napoleon was in contact with many of his old supporters in France and across Europe. He was keeping himself very well informed about events, and was thinking carefully as he laid his plans.

Unrest in France

In Paris discontent was growing. The victorious allies had put Louis XVIII on the throne of France. He was the younger brother of Louis XVI, the king executed during the Revolution. Before allowing him to take his throne, the allies had extracted from Louis promises that he would respect the social and legal changes that had taken place in France since the Revolution, and that he would not engage in any feuds against those who had supported Napoleon. Louis promised everything asked of him, but as soon as he was on the throne he ignored his pledges.

Discontent grew rapidly as new taxes were introduced, officials sacked and new laws repealed. Louis brought back to France thousands of his supporters, who had fled the Revolution. He gave them important positions in government, for which they had no qualifications or skill other than loyalty to Louis. Inefficiency and corruption returned to French government. Soon, it was feared, the old restrictions that had plagued the common people would be reintroduced.

Bad as this was for the long-term prospects of a contented France, of more immediate concern was the behaviour of many of those who had come back to France with Louis. Conscious of their ancient noble blood, resentful of the privileges they had lost and scandalized by the common origins of many who held positions of influence or wealth in the new France, these nobles were favoured by King Louis and lost few opportunities to snub or insult those they considered their inferiors.

Arguments, disputes and fights were frequent. At times they could be politically dangerous. Among the men who had achieved distinction under Napoleon was Michel Ney.

Born the son of a cooper, Ney joined the army in 1787 as a hussar trooper. Under the Revolutionary regime, Ney had gained rapid promotion due to his talent for dashing charges and careful rearguard actions. Napoleon made Ney a Marshal of the army and Duke of Elchingen. When Napoleon abdicated,

Ney was persuaded that France needed his talents and so he accepted high military command from Louis, who in return recognized his dukedom. Other nobles, however, refused Ney the respect due to a duke and made spiteful jokes about his cooper father.

Ney tried to rise above the petty insults and sneers, but his wife felt the insults keenly and would have preferred to return home rather than stay at court. One day, Ney came home to find his wife in tears following a particularly unpleasant insult and social snub from the Duchess of Angoulême – one of the noble ladies most favoured by King Louis. Ney raced to the Tuileries Palace, pushed the guards aside and stormed through the palace seeking the duchess. Passing the king, Ney gave a stiff, formal bow then passed on without saying a word. When he found the duchess, Ney grabbed her arm and shouted, 'While I was fighting for France, you were sipping tea in an English garden.' The Duke of Angoulême intervened and it looked as if Ney was about to floor him with a punch when courtiers restrained him. Calming down, Ney shook off the courtiers and turned to leave. But before he went he pointed at the Angoulêmes and swore 'I'll show you.'

The episode was reported back to Napoleon, along with dozens of other incidents in which returning royal favourites had angered or humiliated those they thought of as their inferiors.

Napoleon also learned that more than 100,000 prisoners of war were returning to France from captivity abroad. These were fully trained veteran soldiers who came home to France to find themselves unemployed and treated with contempt by the new royal officials. Perhaps even worse, the reforms for which they had fought were being dismantled and destroyed. Discontent among these former soldiers was immense. Napoleon knew that they were unhappy and guessed that they would respond willingly to a call to arms to protect and preserve the reforms of the Revolution.

Congress of Vienna

Not content with alienating his own people, Louis was also doing his best to annoy the allies who had put him back on his throne. The diplomats of Europe were meeting in Vienna to draw up a new map of Europe and – just as important – decide on how far the reforms of the Revolution should be allowed to remain standing.

This Congress of Vienna had as its main objective to agree a deal that would ensure peace for the future. Everyone had had more than enough of war. What was needed was an international settlement that would satisfy the ambitions of the big powers, settle any disputes to the satisfaction of anyone important and leave no lingering disagreements to cause problems years into the future.

Adding to the confusion were the myriad border changes that had taken place since the wars began 22 years earlier. Germany had then been composed of nearly 360 separate countries ruled by a bewildering mix of dukes, archdukes, counts, bishops, princes, kings, electors and republics. Some of these states had been little larger than a biggish village, and only a handful were of any real importance.

Nearly all these mini-states had been swept away. Revolutions had done for some, others had been destroyed by the armies of France. Revolutionary France had established reformist republics in its own image, while Napoleon had created equally radical kingdoms ruled by cronies he knew would support his foreign wars. Italy had undergone a similarly radical restructuring.

Not unnaturally, the displaced rulers wanted to be restored to their old positions as rulers. Equally understandably, those who now had control of those lands wanted to hang on to them.

Britain wanted to promote free trade, though nearly all other rulers were against this because they gained a great deal of money from import duties. Having paid for the recruitment and the equipping of most of Europe's armies in order to defeat

France, Britain felt it should be able to recoup some of the money by trade. Nobody else agreed.

Tsar Alexander of Russia declared that the answer to Europe's problems was to accept the social and cultural reforms of the Revolution. This would stop any future revolutions, ensure stability and avoid the need for any political reforms. It soon became clear that Alexander meant that this should be done everywhere except in Russia, where his own autocratic rule would continue unhindered.

Everyone was frightened of France, but all were torn between the desire to weaken France by taking lands away from her and the need to avoid angering France and provoking future trouble.

King Louis decided to pose as the champion of the 'legitimate rulers' and to oppose those who wanted to redraw borders to ensure a balance of power in each region. It was noted, however, that he really made efforts only on behalf of his own allies and friends – while he was willing to compromise his supposedly firm principles over disinheriting others.

Louis demanded that King Frederick Augustus of Saxony be restored to his throne, despite the fact that he had been a staunch ally of Napoleon. This annoyed the Prussians, who were occupying Saxony and had every intention of annexing it. He also wanted to see Parma in Italy restored to its old ruling dynasty, along with Piacenza, Modena and Lucca. That annoyed the Austrians, who were itching to settle these Italian states on relatives of the Austrian Hapsburg dynasty who had remote claims to them. Louis' support for an independent Poland aroused the ire of the Russians because Tsar Alexander thought he had a claim to the Polish throne.

Having annoyed the Russians, Prussians and Austrians, Louis further alienated Russia by denouncing Alexander as a pious-minded simpleton and went on to anger Britain by letting it be known that he expected to get back all the colonies that Britain had captured from France during the long years of war, as well as opposing free trade. Louis' greatest achievement, however, was managing to blame everyone else for his own intransigence.

Indeed, so incendiary were Louis' interventions in the discussions in Vienna that Russia came close to invading Austria over the fate of Poland, while Britain was on the brink of walking out altogether.

Napoleon makes his move

On Elba, Napoleon calculated that the time had come for action. If he delayed much longer, Louis might give way in the face of calls for reform, the unemployed soldiers might find work and the diplomats in Vienna might patch up some form of compromise deal. If he was in any doubt as to what he should do, his mind was made up when a spy at the royal court in Paris brought him news that King Louis' brother, the Count d'Artois, was plotting to have Napoleon murdered.

Towards the end of February, Sir Neil Campbell went to the Italian mainland on business, coincidentally at the same time that British warships stationed at Elba were absent for a few days. Napoleon grabbed his chance. He packed 600 men of his little army on to the brig *Inconstant* – part of Elba's tiny navy. The flag of Elba was hauled down and the tricolour of Revolutionary France raised in its stead.

On 26 March, the *Inconstant* put to sea, heading north-west for France. The following day, it was sighted by the Royal French ship *Zéphir*, flying the white flag sprinkled with gold fleur-de-lis of the royal dynasty. The captain of the *Zéphir* saw that the *Inconstant* was flying the now illegal tricolour and closed to hail and demand an explanation. Nobody on board the *Inconstant* replied and, concerned by the superior armament of the ship, the captain of the *Zéphir* hauled away.

On 1 March, Napoleon and his tiny force landed at Golfe-Juan, then a tiny fishing village but now a holiday resort on the Côte d'Azur. He marched to the town of Antibes, where he was greeted by enthusiastic crowds. He made a speech, which he would repeat at every town he subsequently entered. Napoleon promised to restore the reforms of the Revolution, cut taxes and restore the vote to all adult men. He summoned former soldiers to join his army on a temporary basis to safeguard the new revolution. He also sent out agents to repeat his promises and post up copies of his speech in villages and towns.

It was quickly evident that not everyone was delighted to welcome Napoleon back to France. Several towns in western Provence gave Napoleon's agents a cold reception and some began mustering local militia against him. Knowing that Provence had always been lukewarm about the Revolution, and fearing that a royal army would be marching against him, Napoleon made a decision influenced as much by political as by military considerations.

Instead of taking the main road north up the valley of the Rhône, Napoleon marched his army north through Grasse, Castellane and Gap towards Grenoble – a city long known for its revolutionary and Napoleonic fervour. The route not only took him away from the royalist areas of Provence, it also followed steep, narrow roads that could not be used by artillery. Napoleon had no artillery, but the royal army did. If he was going to meet an enemy army, Napoleon wanted to meet one that did not have large guns.

On 5 March, Napoleon was passing La Mure, with Grenoble only a couple of hours' march away, when he heard that the road ahead was blocked at a defile by the 5th Infantry Regiment. The opposing forces were about equal, though Napoleon had the advantage of having a hundred or so cavalry. The two small armies drew up to face each other. But Napoleon knew that if he were to succeed he would need to do so peacefully. A civil war could end only in his own defeat.

Taking his life in his hands, Napoleon ordered his men to ground arms. He then walked forwards alone and unarmed to face the levelled guns and bayonets of the 5th Regiment. Having got to within 20 metres of the men, Napoleon stopped. He unbuttoned his coat and threw it open to reveal the uniform of his own Imperial Guard.

He declared, 'If any of you soldiers of France wish to kill your emperor, here I am.' There followed a few seconds of tense silence, followed by a shout of '*Vive l'Empereur*' from the ranks of the 5th. Discipline collapsed and the men of the 5th surged forwards to crowd around Napoleon.

The next day another infantry regiment came marching toward Napoleon's army. This time there was no confrontation. Its commander, Charles de la Bédoyère, sent ahead a message saying that he and his men were loyal to Napoleon.

Face to face with Marshal Ney

Meanwhile, a more dangerous force was approaching. When news of Napoleon's arrival in France first reached Paris, the newspaper *Le Moniteur* announced the news with the headline 'The Monster is Loose', followed the next day by 'The Corsican Ogre has landed at Cape Juan'.

King Louis and his government were unconcerned. They had more than 100,000 men under arms, loyalists were in positions of power and influence in the government and Napoleon had a tiny force without artillery. Louis turned to Ney and asked what should be done. 'He should be brought to Paris in an iron cage,' responded Ney, explaining that the last thing that France needed was a civil war. Louis, suffering badly from an attack of gout, appointed Ney to lead a large army south to stop Napoleon's advance and arrest him for treason.

In Vienna, the news of Napoleon's landing in France caused rather more consternation. Britain, Austria, Prussia and Russia all declared war on Napoleon – not on France – and each pledged to put 150,000 men into the field within three months. A command was sent out by the fastest horses available to put the orders into action.

Everyone in Vienna knew that there would be problems with

getting things moving. Britain did not have an army of 150,000 men at all, so its promise would probably be made good by including the navy. The Russian army was dispersed across the vast Russian Empire and would take months to gather; much the same was true of most of the Austrian army. Only the Prussians stood much chance of getting an army to march against France in the near future, and the size of that force was in doubt.

Ney, meanwhile, had gathered his army and had got as far as Auxerre. By 14 March, he was in a distraught frame of mind. He was aware that all along the route north the civilians had cheered Napoleon and local authorities had declared for the emperor. He knew also that several garrisons of troops had likewise declared for Napoleon. Ney had been one of Napoleon's most talented commanders and closest associates, but he had taken service with King Louis and was uncertain how Napoleon might react to such disloyalty. He had been sincere in telling Louis that France could not afford a civil war and that arresting Napoleon was the best way to avoid this, but now he was not so sure. Joining Napoleon might be the surest way to avoid civil war.

Ney talked things over with his officers, then had a letter from Napoleon slipped into his hand. The letter repeated Napoleon's plans as announced in his speeches, then reassured Ney as to his own personal position. 'I will receive you as I did after the Battle of the Moskowa,' it read. The reference was to a celebrated event during the campaign of 1812 when Napoleon had publicly dubbed Ney 'the bravest of the brave'.

Next morning, Ney announced to his army that the true ruler of a country was chosen by its people, not by inheritance. The men cheered and Ney led them to join Napoleon.

Opposite: Napoleon is carried shoulder high into the Tuileries Palace in Paris. His return was widely welcomed by the mass of French citizens who expected him to restore the liberties and freedoms that they had gained in the Revolution.

King Louis concluded that he had chosen unreliable commanders. First de la Bédoyère and now Ney had changed sides. He sent a larger army under the command of his brother the count of Artois and cousin the duke of Orléans to defeat Napoleon. On 19 March, the men and most officers of this army mutinied and declared for Napoleon. Artois and Orléans fled back to Paris and next day King Louis clambered into a coach and raced for the Dutch border.

Back in power – a new constitution

On 20 March, Napoleon entered Paris. The next day, *Le Moniteur* – the same newspaper that had called him a 'monster' and an 'ogre' a fortnight earlier – announced, 'Yesterday evening His Majesty the Emperor made his public entry into our City.'

The Parisian press may have been won over, but Napoleon's enemies were not. The first real trouble came in Provence. The Duke of Angoulême – whose wife had so upset Ney's wife – happened to be in Provence when Napoleon landed and marched north. He quickly mustered a force of men loyal to King Louis and seized a number of towns and key strategic positions – including the great naval base of Toulon. He took his main force as far up the Rhône Valley as the great fortress town of Valence and there awaited relief from the Austrian army mustering in northern Italy.

Those who met Napoleon in Paris could not help noticing that he had put on weight while living on Elba. A few remarked that he was no longer as restive as before, and was prone to periods of sitting around talking or eating. What only a very few people knew was that Napoleon was now suffering from medical problems.

Neither of Napoleon's conditions was especially serious, but both were painful and uncomfortable. The first was that he suffered from periodic bouts of urine retention. More serious for the campaign to come were his haemorrhoids. This condition can be uncomfortable at the best of times, but it made sitting on a horse for more than an hour or so extremely painful. Napoleon had to travel in a coach instead of on horseback. This not only slowed down his movements but also restricted him to good-quality roads.

In the days before radio communications, a military commander needed to be able to travel around the battlefield to see things for himself. Napoleon was not able to do this and consequently was not always fully aware of what was going on.

Such problems were not, however, readily apparent in Paris in March 1815. And Napoleon had other problems.

The most immediately pressing issue was the need to justify his coup and ensure that the move had popular support among the French people. Napoleon therefore called in the constitutional expert Benjamin Constant to draft a new constitution for France. The franchise was expanded to more than three million men immediately, with provision for further expansion. The parliament was to be composed of one chamber of hereditary peers and a second of elected deputies.

The draft constitution – it never got as far as being implemented – guaranteed the freedom of the press and a host of what today would be termed human rights. It also gave to the emperor powers rather more limited than those either Louis XVIII or Napoleon himself had enjoyed before 1814. Napoleon told Constant, 'I am growing old. The repose of a constitutional king may suit me. It will more surely suit my son.'

Dealing with the French royalists

Meanwhile, Napoleon was determined to establish control over all of France, and in particular of the naval base at Toulon. He sent an army south to tackle the Duke of Angoulême. The force was led by Marshal Grouchy, a commander who would play a significant role in the Waterloo campaign.

On 9 April, Grouchy reached Valence and prepared to besiege the city and the Duke of Angoulême. However, Angoulême

EMMANUEL DE GROUCHY

Emmanuel de Grouchy was born in 1766 into one of the premier noble families of France – indeed his grandmother was rumoured to have been a mistress of King Louis XV. He joined the royal army in 1779 as an artillery officer, but a few years later he transferred to the cavalry and joined the royal guard. In the later 1780s Grouchy made several statements supporting the liberal and democratic ideals that would lead to the French Revolution, and was forced to resign from the guards. The new revolutionary government soon brought him back to the army, and by 1793 he had become colonel in command of a regiment of dragoons. He had risen to be a general in command of a cavalry division when he again fell out with the ruler of France – this time arguing fiercely against Napoleon's military coup. Despite this, Napoleon asked Grouchy to return to active service. Although his skill and courage as a cavalry commander were highly acclaimed, Napoleon preferred to use Grouchy in administrative and diplomatic tasks for most of the period 1803–12. Grouchy did, however, command a cavalry division with distinction during the 1812 invasion of Russia and fought gallantly during the terrible Retreat from Moscow.

In 1814, Grouchy was badly injured at the Battle of Craonne. This rather conveniently meant that he avoided making any pledges of loyalty to the restored King Louis, being able to claim he was too ill to journey to Paris. Grouchy's wounds healed suddenly and conveniently in March 1815, allowing him to join Napoleon's army. After the Waterloo campaign, Grouchy fled to the United States of America where he lived until pardoned in 1821. In 1830, under the July Monarchy of the so-called citizen-king Louis Philippe I, he was restored to his military ranks and to his title of Marquis de Grouchy. He lived in retirement until his death in May 1847.

knew that the Austrians had decided to march their main force north to invade France across the Rhine. He was therefore no longer expecting support from the Austrians and opened talks with Grouchy. The two men agreed that Angoulême's men would lay down their arms, but would be free to return home without any reprisals for their action. Delighted to have gained a bloodless victory, Grouchy hurriedly took control of southern France and then returned to Paris. Angoulême, meanwhile, set sail for Britain.

While Grouchy was dealing with Angoulême, a new royalist uprising had begun in the Vendée, in the lower valley of the Loire river. The area had never been particularly keen on the Revolution and had rebelled twice before, in 1792 and 1799. Now the Vendée erupted in a pro-royalist rebellion yet again. The leader was Jean-Baptiste Constant, Count of Suzannet, who had led the 1799 uprising. He was assisted by another local nobleman, Charles de Beaumont, Count of Autichamp. He, too, had fought in the 1799 uprising and, like Suzannet, had subsequently surrendered to Napoleon and been living quietly in retirement. The two men had taken up local government positions on the restoration of Louis XVIII and now saw it as their duty to retain those positions for the king in the face of what they saw as an illegal military coup.

Suzannet and Autichamp captured the town of Cholet and nearby areas without a struggle, but found that very few men rallied to their colours. Only about 8,000 men could be found, and few of them had any real military experience. Unable to advance towards the major towns of the region, the royalists began preparing defensive positions to hold out against the expected Napoleonic offensive.

But the offensive was slow in coming. The royalists were not holding any strategically important areas, so Napoleon felt that he had more important matters to attend to. General Jean Lamarque was sent to the Vendée with 3,000 men. He had orders to recruit men locally to tackle the royalists and to keep them pinned back in their defensive positions, where they could do little harm to Napoleon.

It was not these internal enemies that formed the main threat to Napoleon – it was his foreign foes.

CHAPTER 2

'WHITE KNIGHT TO BLACK BISHOP'

Sir Charles Oman, commenting on Napoleon's ability to mask his intentions

Almost as soon as news arrived in Vienna that Napoleon had landed in France, the war began. The alliance that was hurriedly put together appeared to be impressive indeed. Britain, Russia, Prussia, Austria, Spain, Portugal and a host of smaller German and Italian states all allied themselves against Napoleon. Together they could put nearly one million men into the field. The date for the joint invasion of France was set for 1 July 1815.

In fact, the vast coalition was not as impressive as it appeared to be. The unity of purpose was largely illusory. Only days before, Austria and Russia had nearly gone to war with each other – while Prussia had lingering doubts about British policies and was openly hostile to Austrian claims to leadership of the German-speaking peoples.

Moreover the ability of the allies to put armies into the field was rather in doubt. Some powers were quite unable to do what they had promised. King Ferdinand VII of Spain, for instance, had promised at Vienna to send two armies to invade France. One would go over the eastern Pyrenees to seize Perpignan and Narbonne, the other over the western Pyrenees to take Bayonne and Bordeaux. However, the Spanish government was bankrupt and Spain itself had been badly damaged by eight years of French occupation and wars of liberation. Nobody seriously expected the Spanish army to invade France – at least not in 1815.

'German Corps'

Rather more useful were expected to be the armies of an assort-
ment of smaller states in northern Germany. The Electorate of
Hessen, Grand Duchy of Mecklenburg-Schwerin, Grand Duchy
of Mecklenburg-Strelitz, Grand Duchy of Saxe-Weimar-Eisenach,
Grand Duchy of Oldenburg, Duchy of Saxe-Gotha, Duchy of
Anhalt-Bernburg, Duchy of Anhalt-Dessau, Duchy of Anhalt-
Köthen, Principality of Schwarzburg-Rudolstadt, Principality of
Schwarzburg-Sondershausen, Principality of Waldeck,
Principality of Lippe and the Principality of Schaumburg-Lippe
all promised to muster their armies at Koblenz by early June. It
was expected that they would together total around 25,000 men.

Because none of these small states had a military commander
of note, and in any case were jealous of each other's status,
they asked Prussia to provide a commander. General Friedrich
von Nollendorf was given the task, but he had barely arrived
when he fell dangerously ill and effective command fell to his
second in command, the Hessian general, von Engelhardt.

Engelhardt soon experienced difficulties welding his
confusing array of separate forces into a single army. The
various armies did, at least, all speak the same language but
their system of commands varied dramatically, as did the tactics
in which they were trained. Even more diverse were the
uniforms. The army of Anhalt-Bernburg wore green jackets and
grey trousers. The men of Mecklenburg-Schwerin wore blue
coats and white trousers, except the cavalry who were in green.
The troops of Saxe-Weimar-Eisenach wore white coats with
grey trousers, while those of Anhalt-Bernburg were kitted out
in a fetching shade of sky blue. Making the confusion worse,
the rank badges varied enormously, making it difficult for a
captain from Oldenburg to know if he were supposed to give
orders to an officer from Waldeck or take orders from him.

The task of this 'German Corps' – as it was dubbed – was
to guard the Rhine around Koblenz. When war began in early
July it was expected to advance on the French fortress towns

of Sedan, Bouillon, Montmédy, Laon and Rheims, to which it would lay siege. After capturing those strongpoints, the German Corps was to advance on Paris in co-operation with the Prussian army of Field Marshal Blücher that was forming to its north.

Russian contingents

Other armies were likely to take part, but were certainly going to be late. Tsar Alexander of Russia had promised 250,000 men, with 200,000 men marching immediately and the rest following on in the summer. In fact, it was difficult to know how large these two Russian armies really were. Corruption was widespread and endemic, being considered a normal part of military life. Officers routinely claimed their units were larger than they really were. This enabled them to draw pay and rations for men who did not exist and take it for themselves. It is thought that the First Russian Army may have had an actual strength of about 160,000 men, compared to an official strength of 200,000; but nobody is, or was, certain.

The Russians' military effectiveness was further hampered by their appalling supply system. The supply wagons trundling along behind the troops were empty as often as they were full. More than once in the campaigns of 1812–14 Russian soldiers had been unable to attack due to a total lack of ammunition. Food was also frequently missing, forcing the men to steal and loot to stave off hunger. Whenever civilians learned a force of Russians was approaching they packed everything up and left. What could not be taken away was buried or hidden deep in the forests.

It is indicative of the quality of the Russian army that when Tsar Alexander told Wellington that he could march one advanced army corps to Belgium to arrive by early June, Wellington turned the offer down.

Nevertheless, the First Russian Army was clearly a large force. It was commanded by Field Marshal Barclay de Tolly, who had a distinguished record and was reckoned to be one of the better

Russian field commanders. In order to speed up his advance, Tolly divided his army into three and sent them by different routes across Germany to recombine on the banks of the Rhine near Mainz. This force was expected to reach the Rhine in late June or early July.

Austrians and allies

Also heading for the Rhine was a mixed army of German states under Austrian control. Field Marshal Prince Karl von Schwarzenberg was aged 44 in 1815 and had a solid reputation as a careful military administrator. His reputation as a field commander was so high that he was made the overall commander-in-chief of the Allied armies massing against France. He was generally considered to be a cautious commander who would not advance unless absolutely certain of victory, and would not defend a position unless he understood it fully. Nevertheless, it had been Schwarzenberg who in 1814 had captured Paris, forcing Napoleon's abdication. Together with Austria's key role in the alliance this brought him the supreme command.

As well as around 100,000 Austrian troops, Schwarzenberg had around 150,000 Germans drawn from the Kingdom of Bavaria, Kingdom of Saxony, Kingdom of Württemberg, Grand Duchy of Baden, Grand Duchy of Hesse, Duchy of Saxe-Coburg-Saalfeld, Duchy of Saxe-Meiningen, Duchy of Saxe-Hildburghausen, Free City of Frankfurt and Principality of Reuss.

Schwarzenberg was intending to cross the Rhine near Gemersheim, then advance past Strasbourg and Nancy towards the Seine and Paris. Having captured Paris once before, Schwarzenberg fully intended to capture it again. He had also decided that he would not cross the Rhine in strength until Tolly and the Russians had arrived. In part this may have been his natural caution emerging as a reluctance to face Napoleon alone, but given how close Austria and Russia had come to war just a few weeks earlier it might be that Schwarzenberg wanted to make sure the Russians were invading France, not Austria.

Already in position when the war broke out was the Swiss army of 37,000 men. The commander, General Niklaus von Bachmann, had very firm orders from his government. He was not to move outside Switzerland, no matter what happened. It is indicative of the fraught state of international relations that the Swiss government was uncertain of which foreign power they should be more afraid – the French or the Austrians. Whichever might turn out to be the real enemy, the Swiss were taking no chances. They told their allies that they would keep the French tied down and under observation, though effectively this meant they were not going to join in the invasion of France.

In northern Italy, another Austrian army was gathering under General Johann Frimont, a talented cavalry commander who had fought against Napoleon – though with little success – at Marengo in 1800. Serving under Frimont were the troops of several north Italian states. Other than those from Piedmont, however, it was not entirely certain how reliable these Italian troops were going to be. The Italians had fought alongside the forces of France for years and were known to favour the new freedoms the Revolution had brought them. The return of their autocratic rulers was not generally welcomed, and the soldiers might not be too willing to fight.

Nevertheless, Frimont had around 70,000 men under arms. His orders were to cross the French border on 1 July and secure the pro-royalist areas of Provence, together with the major ports of Toulon and Marseilles, before marching north up the Rhône Valley to Lyons. It was this army that the Duke of Angoulême had been hoping would march to his aid, but it had not – and so the royalist rising in Provence never took off.

Opposite: Joachim Murat in the uniform of a Marshal of France pauses as a squadron of hussars gallops past. Murat was the finest cavalry commander of his day, but lacked political judgement.

Neapolitan War

Frimont had other problems to contend with. When news spread of Napoleon's landing in southern France, southern Italy exploded in a fever of revolutionary fervour. If northern Italy was unreliable for the allies, southern Italy was positively hostile to them. Joachim Murat, King of Naples, wasted no time at all in declaring war on Austria and calling on all Italians to rally to the cause of the freedoms that the revolutionary era had brought them. Austria wanted to reimpose the old rulers, but Murat would kick them out.

Murat began by invading the Papal States with an army of about 50,000 men and 90 cannon. The Pope fled and Murat was welcomed by cheering crowds. He marched on to Ancona, Rimini and Bologna. There were localized outbreaks of rioting and unrest in northern Italy, but Frimont's troops quickly restored order. Frimont sent an army south under General Frederick Bianchi to block Murat's march north. At the Battle of Panaro on 3 April, Murat smashed the Austrian army and marched on into Modena and Florence. Five days later Murat was on the banks of the Po river.

As the situation threatened to spiral out of control, Frimont marched almost his entire army towards Ferrara, then being besieged by Murat. At the Battle of Casaglia on 12 April the fighting was inconclusive, but Murat – suffering supply problems – fell back towards Bologna, then on to Ancona. Murat fought a skilful retreat, but he was outnumbered and handicapped by his lack of supplies. On 20 May, Naples surrendered. There was no sign of Murat. Nobody knew where he had gone.

This Neapolitan War, as it was known, had seriously dislocated Frimont's plans for an invasion of southern France. Most of his army was spread out over Italy, garrisoning unreliable towns and seeking to overawe revolutionaries – and intimidate them into inaction. Without knowing where Murat had gone or what his plans might be, Frimont could not afford to relax.

He gathered as many of his men as he dared in Piedmont, but he was still under strength and was worried about his rear.

Intending to co-operate with Frimont in his invasion of southern France was the British Mediterranean fleet under Lord Exmouth. On board Exmouth's ships were troops of King Ferdinand III of Sicily. Ferdinand was one of the most reactionary monarchs in Europe. He had held on to his throne only because the British fleet backed him in order to retain Sicily as a useful naval base in the central Mediterranean. Nobody, least of all Exmouth, expected much from the Sicilian army.

Some other nations were making token preparations, but with no real prospect of taking part in the coming war. Portugal, for instance, was putting together an army of 14,000 veterans. However, they did not have clearance to march through Spain to reach France, nor had they got the permission of King John VI. John was rather inconveniently on a tour of the interior of Brazil and nobody could get hold of him. Without their monarch's permission the army could not go to war.

The Danish army seemed rather more promising, but it was small and had trouble producing weapons for its men. King Frederick VI thought his forces might be ready to march sometime early in July, though in the event it was the end of that month before they left Denmark.

British and Prussian forces

Of all the armies promised by the allies only two would certainly be ready by the agreed date of 1 July. The first of these was the main Prussian army under the command of Field Marshal Gebhard von Blücher. Blücher had a force of 116,000 men mustered in the Netherlands by early June. He had his headquarters in Namur, but problems with supply and accommodation meant that the army was spread over a large band of territory stretching from Liège to near Charleroi.

The four corps of the Prussian army varied in size between 23,000 and 30,000. Each corps was a balanced body of infantry, cavalry and artillery – in effect, a miniature army. The men were mostly veterans, though there was a large minority of recent recruits. As all the men came from Prussia there was no doubt of their willingness to fight for their king.

Blücher was 73 years old in 1815, but he was fit and active in body and had a sharp mind. He was, moreover, respected by his generals and loved by his men who nicknamed him 'Marshal Forwards' after his favourite command. His aggressive nature was matched by an ability to organize an army with ruthless efficiency. Indeed, as commander of an army, Blücher had only been defeated once – at Lübeck in 1806. Even then Blücher had managed to persuade his French opponent to mount a guard of honour to salute the defeated Prussians.

Also in the Netherlands by early June was an army of 93,000 men under the British Duke of Wellington. Most of these men were British, but there were also substantial allied units. Of these, the most reliable and best trained were probably the King's German Legion. This unit was recruited mostly from Hanoverians, the King of Britain at this date being also the ruler of Hanover. Almost as good were the Brunswickers, led by their duke, Frederick William – known as 'the black duke', due to his swarthy good looks and the jet-black uniforms of his men.

Wellington also commanded the Netherlands troops, led by their prince, William of Orange. Until little over a year earlier the Netherlands had been enthusiastic partisans of Napoleon and the revolutionary reforms. Nobody was entirely certain how reliable they would be in the coming campaign, however.

This large army was, like that of Blücher and for similar reasons, spread out across the western Netherlands. The right-wing units were near Braine-le-Comte, while the left wing was around Brussels.

Unknown to Blücher, Wellington had two orders from the British government to which he had to give absolute priority no matter what the circumstances. The first was to keep the

British part of his mixed army intact. If there was a real possibility of defeat, Wellington was to retreat to the Scheldt Estuary, where the Royal Navy was waiting to evacuate his troops. The British government was aware that the grand alliance was fragile and had no intention of needlessly sacrificing the only large British army in existence. Almost all available troops had been sent to Wellington, and the government was going to need them back for the defence of Britain if everything went badly.

The second priority order was to keep the French king, Louis XVIII, both safe and close to Wellington's headquarters. The post-war government of France had not yet been decided. Some diplomats wanted France to become a republic, arguing that this would at least give stability; others wanted Napoleon's son to take over – the young child would be easily steered by 'advisers' appointed by the allies; others supported Louis. The British government favoured Louis, who for all his faults was the legitimate monarch, and wanted to make sure that he was on the spot in Paris after the war to be able to take power if that is what the allies decided to do.

Napoleon's options

Faced by this impressive mass of armies and states ranged against him, Napoleon soon realized that he had only limited options. By recalling veterans to the colours and mobilizing garrison troops, Napoleon was able to get 198,000 men ready to march by late in May, with 66,000 more being equipped and probably ready by the middle of June. By early July he might have been able to muster as many as 450,000 men. The problem with waiting for these impressive numbers to be gathered, however, was that the allies were bringing up their armies just as rapidly.

Napoleon knew that whenever the fighting began, he was going to be heavily outnumbered by the allies gathering against him. If he stood on the defensive behind France's borders of the Pyrenees, Alps and Rhine he would be able to fight a long defensive campaign, but the final result was hardly in doubt. In the end Napoleon would be defeated. Before that it was likely that there might be a coup back in Paris organized by those who did not want to see France fought over yet again.

If Napoleon was going to win the coming war, he calculated that he had to win a quick, impressive victory that would cow the other allies into making a hasty peace treaty. Knowing as he did the disputes that had been taking place between the allies at the recent Congress of Vienna, Napoleon hoped that a swift victory would reopen these disputes. If he could knock out the Prussian army, for instance, the Austrians might be tempted to occupy Saxony. Such an aggressive move by the Austrians would undoubtedly cause the Russians to fall back to defend their gains in Poland. There might even be war between Russia and Austria.

Napoleon needed a victory – and he needed one quickly. Looking around at his enemies he very quickly reached a decision as to where that victory was to be won.

The Spanish were on the far side of the Pyrenees and had not yet mustered. They could be beaten with ease, but it would be a hollow and unimpressive victory that would not shake the coalition ranged against Napoleon. Much the same reasoning ruled out an attack into northern Italy to defeat the Austro-Italian army commanded by Frimont.

Schwarzenberg's large Austrian army on the Rhine offered possibilities, for if Napoleon could crush an army of 150,000 men or more it would be a real blow to the allies. But that victory by itself would achieve little. With the vast Russian army ponderously rolling west through Germany, Napoleon would have little time to exploit his victory before he would need to fight a second and even more powerful foe.

Rather more tempting were the armies of Wellington and Blücher in the Netherlands. Napoleon knew that a sound defeat of the Prussians might very well split apart the coalition formed against him. Moreover, there were weaknesses in the positions adopted by Wellington and Blücher.

For a start there was no natural barrier protecting the front of the two allies. Frimont had the Alps, Schwarzenberg had the Rhine; but Blücher and Wellington had only the Sambre – a river that was bridged in many places and also had several fords.

Secondly, both armies were scattered across the southern Netherlands (now Belgium). This dispersed disposition had been forced on the armies by the need for supply and billeting, but it meant that the two forces would be slow to concentrate in an emergency.

Third, both Wellington and Blücher had very good cause to be worried about the flanks of their positions, but for opposite reasons. Wellington was supplied from Britain with supplies coming through the Channel ports, principally Antwerp, that lay behind his right flank. A French attack that went to the west around his right flank would cut him off not only from sources of supply but also from any possible line of retreat. Wellington would correctly identify this as being the key weakness of his position.

Blücher, on the other hand, drew his supplies from the east, though Liège and Aachen. In that direction, also, lay his lines of retreat back to Prussia. He would be as worried about his left or eastern flank as Wellington was about his right or western flank. Napoleon could not be certain, but he guessed that neither Wellington nor Blücher could be comfortable where they were: both knew their supply lines and lines of retreat were open to threat if Napoleon made a sudden move.

Even more tempting were the political opportunities. Until only a year before, the area now known as Belgium had been part of France. The allies had taken it away and given it to the Kingdom of the Netherlands. The people of the area were French-speaking and, generally, favoured the reforms of the Revolution. If Napoleon managed to drive the allies out of the area – or even just march into the largest city, Brussels, amidst popular rejoicing – it would send political shockwaves across Europe, stirring up revolutionaries and causing the more reactionary rulers to pull their troops home to secure their thrones.

Just as critical were the respective strengths of the two Allied armies. Together they outnumbered Napoleon's forces, but separately they were each outnumbered by Napoleon. If Napoleon could separate Blücher and Wellington then attack each in turn, he could bring his temporary superior strength to bear and defeat them both. Napoleon knew that Blücher preferred to attack, while Wellington preferred to defend – and he planned his strategy accordingly.

Attack in the Netherlands

The opportunity for which Napoleon was looking came in the first week of June when the disposition of the Allied armies shifted somewhat. Wellington moved his left-wing units back towards Brussels, while at the same time Blücher moved his right-wing units slightly towards Namur. This opened up a small gap between the two armies. In itself this might not have been crucial, but the gap was at the town of Charleroi, a key position where many roads met and where there were good bridges over the river Sambre.

If Napoleon grabbed Charleroi he would have put his army between those of Wellington and Blücher. He could, therefore, attack whichever one he wanted to destroy first before the other had a realistic chance of concentrating its forces from its dispersed billets and getting into action. Knowing that Blücher was more likely to attack aggressively than was Wellington, Napoleon decided to destroy the Prussian army first.

Having decided to fight the decisive battle in the Netherlands, Napoleon had to arrange his own deployments. In this he was aided by Marshal Louis-Nicolas Davout, arguably the finest French commander of the period – after Napoleon himself.

When Davout took up his position as minister of war a few days after Napoleon's return he had no idea where the decisive battle might be fought, but guessed it would be either on the Rhine or in the Netherlands.

It had been the French who had first developed the corps system, and Davout now organized Napoleon's growing army into 12 corps, together with a cavalry reserve and the Imperial Guard. Each corps was a complete army in miniature composed of infantry, cavalry and artillery with its own supply system, staff and command structure. Each corps could, therefore, operate quite independently, or could join with other corps to form a larger army.

The first six corps were all substantial forces commanded by experienced and talented marshals of France, and were all stationed in north-eastern France. The I Corps, under d'Erlon, was at Lille. The II Corps, commanded by Reille, was at Valenciennes. Vandamme was with the III Corps at Rocroi. The IV Corps under Gérard was at Metz. The V Corps, commanded by Rapp, was at Strasbourg. The VI Corps, under Lobau, was near Laon. The cavalry reserve was likewise in north-eastern France, at Guise, while the Imperial Guard was in Paris under Napoleon's personal command.

The other bodies of the French army being assembled by Davout were all considerably smaller. The VII Corps, also known as the Army of the Alps, was commanded by Marshal Louis-Gabriel Suchet. It was made up of about 15,000 men, about half of whom were drawn from the National Guard, not the regular army. It was based at Lyons and had the task of watching the passes over the Alps from Switzerland and Italy.

The Army of the Jura was commanded by General Claude Lecourbe and composed of only about 6,000 men, again half of whom were from the National Guard. Lecourbe was to watch the Swiss, but to take no offensive action.

Another 5,000 men made up the Army of the Var, based at Toulon and commanded by Marshal Guillaume Brune. His task was to stop any further uprisings by the royalists of the Provence region.

Some 3,000 men made up the Army of the Eastern Pyrenees at Toulouse, while a similar-sized Army of the Western Pyrenees was at Bordeaux. Both forces had the task of watching the Spanish border to stop any incursions from that direction.

Finally, the Army of the West was made up of 10,000 men under General Jean Lamarque. Their task was to put down a royalist rising in the lower Loire valley that was proving to be rather troublesome.

Davout was also supervising the mustering and equipping of more troops, drawing on both the returning prisoners of war and on new recruits. These men were being drawn from all corners of France, but were being moved towards Paris where they could act as a central reserve. The numbers were growing steadily so that by the first week of June Davout had 20,000 men with more arriving daily.

Having decided to launch a swift offensive into the Netherlands, Napoleon had Davout form a new Army of the North. This army was to be made up of I Corps, II Corps, III Corps, IV Corps, VI Corps, the cavalry reserve and the Imperial Guard. This gave him a total force of 130,000 men, the vast majority of them veterans and all of them fully equipped and well supplied. Napoleon deliberately kept these corps dispersed at the main bases until the last possible moment. He guessed that the allies had spies in France and wanted to give them as little advance warning of his intention to attack as possible. It was not until 6 June that the first units began to march for the rendezvous at Avesnes. Napoleon himself stayed in Paris, ostentatiously attending social and routine government meetings, until 3 am on 12 June. The concentration of the Army of the North was at Avesnes on the afternoon of 13 June. After 24 hours' rest, the army marched.

Missing from the French deployment

There were, however, three key men not present with Napoleon as the army headed north to face battle.

The first was Joachim Murat, recently ousted as King of Naples. A couple of weeks after vanishing from Naples he had arrived in Marseilles, having eluded the British naval blockade by disguising himself as a Sardinian fisherman. On arrival, he sent a message to Napoleon asking how he could be of service. Napoleon sent back a message welcoming Murat to France, but giving him no work to do. This was odd. Murat was the finest cavalry commander not just of his generation but of the entire 19th century. He had proved his loyalty, courage and skill in battle after battle the length and breadth of Europe. Yet Napoleon left him kicking his heels while less talented men commanded corps and armies.

Also missing was Marshal Ney. Like Murat, Ney was a talented commander who was enormously popular with the rank and file of the French army. Ney was skilled at co-ordinating cavalry, infantry and artillery and was a dogged and tenacious commander who had kept Napoleon's rearguard together during the horrific retreat from Moscow in 1812. In 1814 it had been Ney who had been instrumental in persuading Napoleon to abdicate as emperor and, although Ney had been among the first to join Napoleon in 1815, he had not been properly forgiven. Like Murat he was treated well, but given no work to do.

The third missing figure was, arguably, the most important: Marshal Louis-Alexandre Berthier. From 1795 to 1814 Berthier had been continuously at Napoleon's side. He was the Imperial Chief of Staff, the man responsible for the crucial staff work that converted Napoleon's intentions into battlefield reality. Berthier's tasks involved keeping maps showing which bridges could support artillery and supply wagons, and which could cope with only infantry. He knew how many wagons were needed to keep an infantry division supplied, and how many were needed for a cavalry corps. Most important, he knew how to convert Napoleon's often brusque and generalized verbal orders into polite and precise written orders for the generals to follow.

Unlike Murat and Ney, Berthier was sent for by Napoleon. Unfortunately the emperor's return to France caught Berthier on a visit to Bamberg in Bavaria. The Bavarians put him under house arrest. A few weeks later a column of Prussian troops marched through Bamberg and that very same day Berthier died when he fell out of the attic window of the house where he was staying. The Prussian general announced that Berthier had been so upset by the sight of Prussians marching to invade France that he had committed suicide. Very few people believed the story and it is widely believed that the Prussians murdered him.

Movements before battle

That night the French army camped close to the Netherlands border, all units carefully positioned to the south of woods or hills so that their campfires would not be seen by the Allied cavalry scouts to the north. The ruse worked in part, but Prussian piquets saw the glow of the fires near Beaumont. Prussian scouts on their left flank noticed that the French outposts that had been visible for the past two weeks were gone. Pushing cautiously forward for more than 3 km they found only abandoned French camps. The French troops had moved somewhere else.

Another item of news that reached the Prussian outposts that night came from a Dutch farmer who was hurrying home to get away from the large French army. He could not give a reliable estimate of numbers, but he did pass on the news that Napoleon was there in person.

Opposite: The positions of the armies in early June 1815. Napoleon had left as few men as he dared watching other sections of the French frontier while he concentrated his main force to attack Wellington and Blucher in the Netherlands.

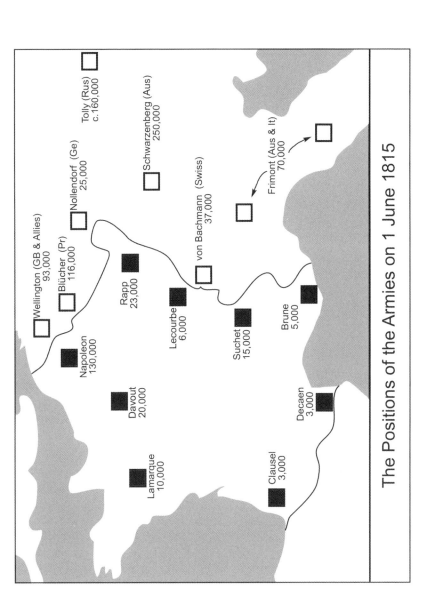

The Positions of the Armies on 1 June 1815

Wellington (GB & Allies)
93,000

Blücher (Pr)
116,000

Nollendorf (Ge)
25,000

Tolly (Rus)
c.160,000

Schwarzenberg (Aus)
250,000

Frimont (Aus & It)
70,000

von Bachmann (Swiss)
37,000

Napoleon
130,000

Rapp
23,000

Davout
20,000

Lecourbe
6,000

Lamarque
10,000

Suchet
15,000

Brune
5,000

Decaen
3,000

Clausel
3,000

The Army of the North was divided into three for the march north to ease congestion on the roads – particularly for the artillery. On the left flank, marching by way of Solre-sur-Sambre, were I and II Corps – about 44,000 men. In the centre, going through Beaumont, were the 60,000 men of III and VI Corps, the Imperial Guard and the Cavalry Reserve. On the right was IV Corps – 16,000 men.

Dawn the next day came clear and bright, promising good campaigning weather. The officers of every unit had been issued overnight with a proclamation from Napoleon that they were to read out to their troops as the units paraded before marching off. It read as follows:

'Soldiers: This day is the anniversary of Marengo and Friedland, which twice decided the destiny of Europe. Then, as after the battles of Austerlitz and Wagram, we were too generous. We believed in the protestations and oaths of princes to whom we left their thrones. Now, however, leagued together, they strike at the independence and sacred rights of France. They have committed unjust aggressions. Let us march forward and meet them; are we not still the same men? Soldiers: At Jena, these Prussians, now so arrogant, were three to one; at Montmirail six to one. Let those who have been captive to the English describe the nature of their prison ships, and the sufferings they endured. The Saxons, the Belgians, the Hanoverians, the soldiers of the Confederation of the Rhine, lament that they are obliged to use their arms in the cause of princes who are the enemies of justice, and the destroyers of the rights of nations. They well know the coalition to be insatiable. After having swallowed up twelve millions of Poles, twelve millions of Italians, one million of Saxons, and six millions of Belgians, they now wish to devour the States of the second order among the Germans. Madmen! One moment of prosperity has bewildered them. To oppress and humble the people of France is out of their power; once entering our territory, there they will find their doom. Soldiers: We have forced marches before us, battles to fight and dangers to encounter; but firm in resolution, victory must be ours. The honour and happiness of our country are at stake! And, in short, Frenchmen, the moment is arrived when we must conquer or die!'

The man responsible for guarding the frontier at the spot where Napoleon was about to cross into the Netherlands was Hans von Zieten, who commanded the Prussian I Corps. Throughout the daylight hours of 14 June Zieten received a series of rather vague reports. None of these in themselves was conclusive, but taken together they indicated very strongly that the main French army was to his south and was about to advance.

Several local farming families arrived on carts, seeking safety from what they said was a vast French army. Men came driving sheep, cattle and horses that they were likewise taking to safety. A couple of deserters from the French army came over the border, claiming to be ardent royalists who had been conscripted by force. They said that Napoleon was leading an army of 150,000 men and intended to capture Brussels.

In the mid afternoon, Zieten passed on the reports to both Blücher and Wellington. However, he emphasized that all these reports came from unreliable sources, that his own scouts had seen nothing unusual and that he could not be sure either where Napoleon was concentrating his army or where he was going to lead it. A French offensive into the Netherlands within the next few days did, however, seem to be highly likely.

At about 7 pm several of Zieten's forward cavalry scouts reported that they had seen columns of men, artillery and wagons heading north along roads near Beaumont and Philippeville. The estimates of the numbers of men involved varied, but all scouts put the numbers in the tens of thousands.

At this date the estimation of troop types and numbers by scouts was of crucial importance. Light cavalrymen underwent lengthy training programmes to enable them to make good estimations. They were expected to be able to tell the difference between dust clouds kicked up by infantry, cavalry and carts at distances of up to 25 km in clear conditions. On sunny days the amount of sunlight sparkling on weapons, belt buckles and horse harnesses would give an indication of the numbers of men on the move. On overcast nights the light reflected from clouds would indicate the number of campfires alight. Estimates of troop types and movement given by light cavalrymen were usually reliable.

By dusk on 14 June Zieten had a good idea of how many Frenchmen were on the march and where they were going. He sent gallopers off to both Blücher and Wellington announcing the news.

Blücher had the news by 10 pm and at 11 pm a string of gallopers went out carrying his orders to the commanders of the Prussian Corps. They were to gather at Sombreffe, a village on the main road from Namur to Nivelles where there was a junction, with a side road going to Charleroi. Zieten, however, was to stay where he was and keep an eye on the French moving to his front.

Trying to out-think Napoleon

Blücher had faced Napoleon before and knew him to be a master of manoeuvre. One of Napoleon's greatest victories had been won almost without firing a shot. In October 1805 Napoleon was facing the Austrian commander Mack von Leiberich on the Danube near Ulm in Bavaria. Napoleon marched around 80,000 men into view of the Austrian scouts, but kept some 40,000 men out of sight. Studying Napoleon's movements, Mack concluded that the French were going to try to work around the right flank of his army of 60,000 men to cut him off from Vienna. Mack therefore spent the next two days watching Napoleon's slow advance while preparing elaborate defences on the right to stop the French.

Napoleon, however, had meanwhile sent most of his army in the opposite direction and by a series of rapid, lengthy marches managed to get behind Mack's defences before the Austrians realized that Napoleon was not where they thought he was. Over the next five days, Napoleon hustled Mack from one untenable position to another until he was trapped with his back to the Danube without food, ammunition or hope of relief. Mack surrendered his entire army. Napoleon lost only 500 men.

At Austerlitz, Napoleon with 67,000 men had faced a joint

Austro-Russian army of 86,000. Napoleon spent most of 1 December 1805 manoeuvring his army in full view of the enemy, apparently intending to attack the next morning on the right flank of the Austro-Russians where the land was open and suitable for cavalry charges. That night, under cover of darkness, the Russians secretly moved their main force from the hills in their centre to their right to meet Napoleon's attack.

This was, in fact, exactly what Napoleon had wanted. During the night he had moved his main force to the centre. At dawn, he launched a massive assault up the hills, smashed the Russian centre then wheeled to take their right wing in the rear. Taken by surprise in flank and rear the Austro-Russians fled. Few managed to get far, for Napoleon's cavalry swooped on them. Napoleon lost 1,305 men dead. The Austro-Russians lost 16,000 dead and 22,000 taken prisoner.

These sorts of cunningly concealed manoeuvres were typical of Napoleon. It was almost axiomatic that what he seemed to intend to do was not what he would actually do. One commentator compared the connection between Napoleon's intentions and his actions as 'white knight to black bishop'. By concentrating his forces at Sombreffe, Blücher was hoping to keep his options open. The roads would allow him to move east, west or north depending on what Napoleon was doing.

Wellington was equally wary of committing his troops until he knew what Napoleon was actually up to. He remained concerned that Napoleon would seek to work around his right flank to cut the British off from the English Channel. Wellington sent out orders that all units should be ready to march at short notice with full equipment, but he did not move any unit.

LOUIS-NICOLAS DAVOUT

Davout was born into a family of the lower nobility and joined the Royal French army just before the Revolution as a cavalry lieutenant. His noble birth got him into some minor trouble, but his skills saw him through and by 1792 he was a brigadier general. Davout's marriage to a pretty girl named Aimée Leclerc turned out to be highly advantageous as her brother was married to the sister of another young general – Napoleon Bonaparte. As Napoleon rose, so did Davout. His organizational skills were matched by his tactical ability: at Auerstädt in October 1806, for instance, he defeated a Prussian army of 63,000 with only 28,000 men.

In 1807, Napoleon burnished his revolutionary credentials when he created the Duchy of Warsaw out of Polish-speaking lands belonging to the defeated Prussia. The new state had an impeccably democratic constitution under which serfdom and other medieval restrictions were abolished. Davout, however, was put in place as Governor General to command the army and keep it loyal to Napoleon. After the failure of the 1812 invasion of Russia, Davout was moved to command the fortified city of Hamburg. He was still there, holding out against overwhelming odds, in 1814 and surrendered only when he learned Napoleon had abdicated. When Napoleon returned to power, Davout was summoned to become Minister of War, though many felt that he should have gone on campaign where his skills would have been of more direct use. After Waterloo, Louis XVIII sacked Davout and stripped him of all his titles and privileges. By 1819, he was back in favour. He died in 1823, leaving his titles and estates to the appropriately named Napoleon Davout.

Chapter 3

'Humbugged me, by God!'

Wellington to the Earl of Malmesbury, 15 June 1815

As dusk fell on 14 June the Prussian commander of I Corp, Zieten, ordered his men to sleep in their uniforms and with their weapons within reach. Additional outposts were pushed forward and officers told to rouse their men an hour before dawn. He was expecting to be attacked and was determined not to be taken by surprise.

Wellington went to sleep in a calmer state of mind. Unknown to his allies, or indeed nearly all his own commanders, Wellington had sent his top spy south of the French border. Lieutenant-Colonel Colquhoun Grant was riding in uniform – so that he would not be shot if captured – but he was co-ordinating a mass of royalist sympathizers who could move freely about northern France. Wellington had relied upon Grant during the Peninsular War, and he was depending on him again now. Wellington had learned to trust no intelligence, no matter how outwardly impressive, unless Grant had approved it. Now Wellington would not move until he had word from Grant.

On the evening of 14 June the long-awaited message from Grant arrived. It was accurate in every detail, giving Napoleon's strength and the road he was taking towards Brussels. The message arrived at the Hanoverian cavalry outposts of General von Dornberg's division on Wellington's far right flank. Dornberg passed the message on promptly but, not realizing the significance, omitted to state that the message had come from somebody called Grant. When the message arrived at Wellington's headquarters it was added to the pile of incoming reports from scouts. In all likelihood, Wellington never even saw it.

Only a few days before, Wellington and Blücher had met and discussed despatches from their superior, Schwarzenberg. These had reviewed the latest intelligence and scouting reports. It was generally agreed that Napoleon would behave as he had done in 1814 when defending France and launch a pre-emptive strike across the upper Rhine. Militarily, it was the sensible thing to do. Blücher and Wellington had separated, agreeing that they would invade France together once Napoleon had attacked on the Rhine. By the evening of 14 June nothing had happened to change their minds.

Around 3 am, soldiers in a Prussian outpost were surprised to find themselves approached by three French officers. The surprise grew greater when the officers turned out to be General Louis de Bourmont and two colonels. Bourmont brought with him a copy of Napoleon's orders to his army for the next few days. He was taken to see Blücher, who instead of welcoming Bourmont called him a traitor to his face. Blücher's Chief of Staff, August von Gneisenau, stepped in to remind Blücher that Bourmont now wore the royalist white cockade in his hat and was therefore an ally.

'Cockade be damned,' shouted Blücher. 'A dirty dog is a dirty dog.' He threw Bourmont out of his headquarters and refused to see him again.

Despite his anger, Blücher had gained from Bourmont's defection. He now knew beyond doubt that Napoleon and his main army were marching into the Netherlands. What he did not know was quite what Napoleon's intentions were.

Hearing of the desertion, Napoleon made some changes to his plans, but the overall pattern could not be altered substantially as the men were already marching.

The fighting begins
The first shots were fired at 3.30 am when French advanced scouts made contact with outposts of Zieten's corps. At about

4.30 am Zieten himself heard the rumble of distant cannon fire at his headquarters. The noise was coming from the south and, after spending some time trying to pinpoint the source of the noise more accurately, Zieten sent messengers to Blücher and Wellington announcing that his outposts were being attacked and that, should the attack turn out to be serious, he would fall back towards Fleurus.

Although Zieten could not be certain, the cannon were in fact French guns firing directly south of Charleroi. They marked the French assault on Zieten's most southerly units as they marched directly north to seize Charleroi.

When Blücher received Zieten's report at about 10.30 am, he sent out messages ordering his corps commanders to hurry up and get to Sombreffe as fast as possible. One of those orders – to von Bülow, the commander of the Prussian IV Corps – was to cause massive confusion. An earlier order had told Bülow to march his corps to Hannut, a few miles to the north-east of Sombreffe. This was probably to prevent the Prussian army congesting the roads, but Bülow had managed to convince himself that the entire Prussian army was going to gather at Hannut.

Matters were not helped by the fact that Bülow outranked Blücher's Chief of Staff, Gneisenau, and was notoriously prickly about status. Rather then write the sort of blunt order he would address to other officers, therefore, Gneisenau had couched his message to Bülow as a request. Bülow completely failed to gather from this message that there was any urgency at all. Not realizing that Napoleon was attacking, Bülow continued to Hannut and spent the night there.

Bülow sent a message to Blücher informing him of what he was doing. Blücher fired off an angry response telling Bülow to march to Gembloux to join up with the rest of the Prussian army.

Opposite: Blucher (left) and Wellington met early on the morning of 16 June before the battles of Ligny and Quatre Bras, but then did not meet again until 9 pm as the main battle of Waterloo drew to a close.

This confused Bülow even more. In the event he let his men sleep and did not move until the morning of 16 June.

Zieten's message to Wellington arrived at a little after 9 am. Wellington was frustrated by the rather vague nature of the message. Cannon were firing somewhere south of Zieten's headquarters. That could mean anything. Still concerned about his communications to the Channel ports, and having received no message from the spy Grant, Wellington sent urgent messages to his own forward units asking for news of any enemy movements to their front. Crucially, for the first time, this message told his forward commanders to tell him instantly if a message arrived from somebody called Grant. Unfortunately, when the message reached Dornberg, who had earlier received a report from Grant, it was merely logged by his staff.

A regiment of hussars of the King's German Legion sent back a report of a party of French cavalry probing north near Mons towards the right flank of Wellington's position. This caused Wellington real concern. Was Napoleon merely feinting toward Charleroi while the real attack would be toward the Channel ports? In fact, the French cavalry were a strong force sent by Napoleon to find out if Wellington was still in position or if he had moved to join Blücher.

Zieten was, meanwhile, organizing a fighting retreat. As he had earlier decided, he fell back toward Fleurus. This town lay between Blücher's headquarters at Namur and Wellington's at Brussels. He could, therefore, continue to act as a link between the two main armies. At 11 am Zieten abandoned Charleroi and its important road junction. There then followed a pause while the French main body got over the river Sambre, resuming their advance at 3 pm.

It was at about this time that a wounded Prussian cavalryman arrived at Quatre Bras, a crossroads where the Namur–Nivelles road crosses that from Charleroi to Brussels. There he found the 2nd Nassau Regiment peacefully encamped and entirely unaware that any fighting was taking place at all. The Nassau Regiment was part of the Netherlands army, which was under Wellington's command. Major Philip von Normann of the Nassauers listened to what the Prussian had to say. He then sent a galloper off to Brussels to give Wellington the news, pushed scouts south toward Charleroi and drew his men up for battle. The man riding to Brussels passed several other units of the Netherlands army and told them his news.

News of the fighting had meanwhile arrived at the headquarters of the Dutch army. Their commander was Prince William of Orange, later to become King William II of the Netherlands. Prince William had served in the British army for two years from 1811 to 1813, mostly on active service in the Peninsular War under Wellington. His jovial nature and calm courage under fire won him many admirers in the British army. He was, however, still only 23 years old during the Waterloo Campaign and comparatively inexperienced.

Having interviewed the scouts who had seen the French around Charleroi, Prince William leapt on his horse and, with a small escort, spurred north to tell Wellington what was going on. Arriving in Brussels, William found Wellington at about 5 pm and blurted out his news. Wellington listened patiently, then asked some questions. Prince William's news did not really add very much to what he already knew. The French were attacking near Charleroi but in numbers that might add up to only a single corps. The location of the bulk of Napoleon's army was still unknown. The Prince of Orange rode back to his headquarters to discover more news.

Wellington's orders

Nevertheless, Wellington decided it was time to take action. The messages were written by Wellington's aide, Sir William de Lancey, and sent out by courier. The messages were clear, but cautious. All divisions were to gather together immediately and be ready to march at dawn next day.

At 6 pm scouting parties of French lancers appeared in front of Normann's Nassauers south of Quatre Bras. Skirmishing followed, forcing Normann to fall back to the crossroads. A Netherlands battery of cannon arrived at this point and opened fire, driving the lancers away. The cannon fire was heard by Prince Bernhard of Saxe-Weimar, who at once marched his three regiments towards the sound of gunfire. He arrived at Quatre Bras at about 8 pm and took command of the situation. By nightfall he had with him a mixed force of Dutch and Brunswick troops that together made up about half a division in strength.

Among the men who received Wellington's orders was Count Perponcher, who commanded the 2nd Netherlands Division – of which both Normann and Saxe-Weimar were a part. His orders told him to collect his men at Nivelles and be ready to march at dawn next day. Only a short time earlier, however, Perponcher had received messages from Saxe-Weimar outlining the situation at Quatre Bras. He recognized the strategic importance of the crossroads and concluded that it was his duty to try to hold it. He ignored the direct orders of Wellington, reasoning that Wellington must have issued his orders before he heard of events at Quatre Bras. Instead of gathering his division at Nivelles, he mustered it at Quatre Bras.

At the same time none of the Prussian corps were where Blücher wanted them to be. The II Corps was camping about about 10 km from Sombreffe, the III Corps about 25 km away and Bülow's unfortunate IV Corps was 100 km away. Zieten's I Corps was closest – at Fleurus; but his men were tired after a long day of a fighting retreat. In fact the only Prussians at Sombreffe were Blücher himself and his headquarters staff.

Opposite: The southern Netherlands in 1815. The main road running north from Charleroi through Quatre Bras and Waterloo to Brussels was wide and well paved. Most other roads on this map were made of gravel which were pounded by thousands of hooves and feet, slowing movement.

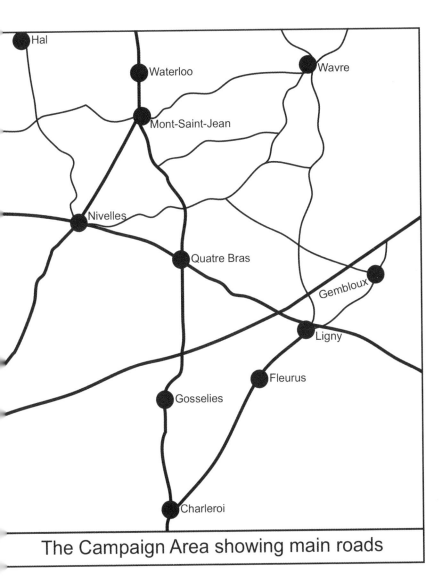

The Campaign Area showing main roads

Dancing in Brussels

Wellington was at this point arriving in his finest evening clothes at a ball being given by the Duchess of Richmond. The ball had been arranged some days in advance, and Wellington had made it clear that he wanted it to go ahead. The last thing he wanted was for panic to spread among the civilians of Brussels. Fear would achieve nothing, and if the civilians fled they would block the roads that Wellington was going to need for his army. Whatever else happened, Wellington was determined to give the impression that everything was perfectly normal.

Soon after the ball began, the Prussian liaison officer, General Karl von Müffling, arrived with detailed news of events from Blücher. The message had been written at noon and gave detailed descriptions of what Blücher knew of the events so far. This was the first time that Wellington was made aware that the main French body was crossing the river Sambre at Charleroi. Wellington retired to a side room to read the despatches and discuss them with his senior officers.

A few minutes later orderlies began to rush off, carrying messages to various regiments in their camps scattered across the countryside around Brussels. Some units were to march at once towards Nivelles, others were to come to Brussels, others were to be ready to march at dawn but to await further orders before moving.

When Wellington himself emerged, he was approached by the elderly Earl of Malmesbury, who asked what was happening. 'Napoleon is at Charleroi,' Wellington replied. 'He has humbugged me, by God. He has gained twenty-four hours' march on me.'

Next to talk to Wellington was the Duchess of Richmond, who asked if she should stop the ball. Wellington appeared shocked. 'No', he replied. 'All officers obliged to ladies will finish their dances. There is no cause for alarm.'

There was, in fact, very good reason for alarm. Napoleon had gained the first victory of the campaign by getting between Wellington and Blücher. Napoleon was in a position to turn on Blücher and defeat him before Wellington could intervene. Wellington now accepted that Napoleon was invading the Netherlands with his main army, but he was still unconvinced that an assault up the main road to Brussels was really what Napoleon was up to. Wellington suspected that this was merely a feint. He still wanted to hear from Grant. A little after midnight Wellington went to bed.

Müffling wrote a report to Blücher stating that Wellington was concentrating his army at Nivelles and gave an estimate of what time particular units would be arriving there.

At 2 am Wellington was woken by a knock at his bedroom door. De Lancey put his head around the door and announced the arrival of the Brunswick cavalry commander Dornberg with news. Dornberg had finally read the message issued that morning instructing him to be alert for news from Grant. Dornberg at once realized that he had passed on Grant's message the day before without saying who it was from. He had leapt into the saddle and ridden as fast as he could to Brussels to report and apologize to Wellington.

Wellington leapt from his bed and dashed to his office, still in his night shirt. He studied the map, then told de Lancey to order the entire army to march on Quatre Bras as quickly as possible. Senior officers were to be roused from their sleep and dragged to Wellington's office. The need for speed was now paramount.

Marshal Ney – and French movements

As Wellington realized what a mess he was in, from the French point of view things looked very good indeed. The march north was going well, and if it was falling slightly behind schedule that did not seem to be very serious. Napoleon's cavalry had reported at lunchtime that Wellington had not yet moved his army. Indications were, however, that Blücher was concentrating his forces somewhere beyond Fleurus. That suited Napoleon very well. If Blücher's army was gathered together it could be destroyed before Wellington's had gathered and could march to help. About lunchtime on 14 June, there was a new arrival at Napoleon's mobile headquarters, at that point situated just outside Charleroi. This was Marshal Michel Ney. As he rode into the camp, there were shouts and cheers from the soldiers as they recognized one of their favourite and most respected commanders.

It had been Ney who had advised King Louis to imprison Napoleon in an iron cage, and before that it had been Ney who had persuaded Napoleon to abdicate in 1814. His subsequent decision to join Napoleon as the emperor marched on Paris had done nothing to disarm Napoleon's apparent distrust. The highly talented Marshal of France had been given no job to do. It was not until Napoleon had been leaving Paris that he had sent Ney a message telling him to hurry up and join his emperor if he wanted to be present at the first battles.

The message had given Ney no clue as to what – if anything – Napoleon would want Ney to do. Ney had thought to bring with him his favourite staff officer, Colonel Heymes, but had not had time to get his proper campaign steeds and arrived to see Napoleon mounted on a borrowed horse.

Napoleon greeted Ney with the words, 'Bonjour, Marshal Ney. I want you to take command of my I and II Corps. Then you must go to Quatre Bras, drive away any enemy troops you find there and open up the main road to Brussels.' Ney was amazed, but delighted. Pausing only to get hold of a proper cavalry horse and to collect an escort of light cavalry to act as bodyguard and messengers, Ney rode off.

As Ney left he had little idea where d'Erlon's I Corps or Reille's II Corps actually were. His first job was to find out, then lead them to Quatre Bras. He soon found d'Erlon at Jumet

Opposite: In the early hours of 16 June, Wellington rushed from his bed in Brussels to order the entire army to march on Quatre Bras.

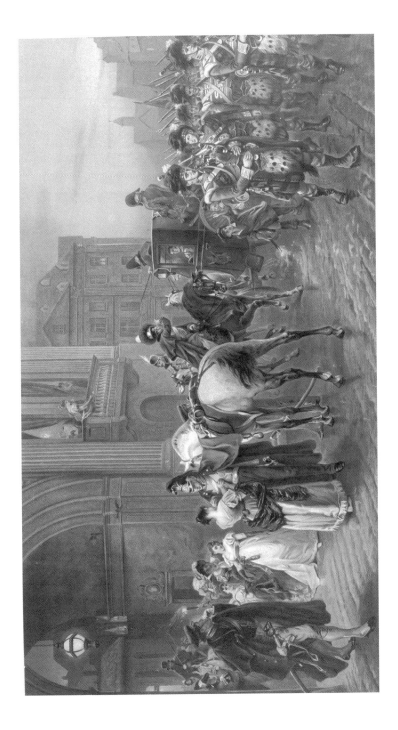

but found that much of his corps was spread out on the march. Ney issued orders to close up the troops into a more compact body and march to Quatre Bras. He sent out numerous messengers to try to find Reille. Napoleon had also given Ney the III Cavalry Corps, but they would not join him until late the following day.

Ney himself reached Quatre Bras at almost 10 pm. It was getting dark and he could not see the enemy position clearly.

The French officers already there told him that the enemy was present with about one division of infantry plus a few guns and a small number of cavalry. Realizing that he could do nothing until daylight and reinforcements arrived, Ney went to Gosselies to sleep and await news of Reille.

Napoleon had, meanwhile, put Marshal Grouchy in command of the right wing of the French army. That meant Grouchy had the III Corps (Vandamme), IV Corps (Gérard), I Cavalry Corps and II Cavalry Corps. Napoleon kept under his own command, as a central reserve, VI Corps (Lobau), IV Cavalry Corps and the Imperial Guard. His orders to Grouchy were to drive back the Prussians of Zieten's corps – and any others they meet – as far as Sombreffe.

Grouchy's advance proved to be slower than Napoleon wanted due to the larger than expected size of the Prussian rearguard. By nightfall, Grouchy had got only as far as halfway between Fleurus and Ligny. Napoleon was not too upset, however, for all the reports indicated that a large part of the Prussian army was at Ligny, where it was isolated from Wellington and ripe for destruction.

At midnight Ney, Grouchy and Napoleon dined together in Charleroi. It turned out to be an unfortunate event for the French. Napoleon chose to criticize Ney for some of the minor movements he had made with his advanced units. Grouchy came away with the impression that Napoleon had been angry because Ney had not done exactly as ordered. He decided that he would do as ordered in future.

Napoleon told Ney and Grouchy that he would decide what to do next day as soon as the situation became clear. The two marshals left for their own headquarters and got some sleep. There would be a battle next day and they needed to be fresh.

Marshal Ney

Michel Ney was born the son of a retired soldier in Sarrelouis, then in France but now in Germany, in 1769. The house where he was born is now a café bearing his name. After leaving school, Ney became a civil servant, but in 1787 ran off to join the army as an hussar. He advanced rapidly through the ranks and was a sergeant when he fought at the Battle of Valmy in 1792, where a Prussian invasion was halted.

Ney was an ardent supporter of the ideals of the Revolution, which helped him to be commissioned as an officer soon after Valmy, and just four years later he attained the rank of general. He led several successful cavalry actions in the years that followed, being wounded several times and captured once – though he was exchanged for an Austrian general soon after. In 1804, he was one of the first officers to be created Marshal of the Empire by Napoleon and thereafter was one of Napoleon's favourite commanders.

In 1807, it was Ney's timely arrival at Eylau that saved Napoleon from almost certain defeat at the hands of a Russian–Prussian alliance. Ney was then sent to Spain against Wellington, where he achieved some successes against the Spanish and Portuguese. He faced Wellington at Busaco in 1810 where he won something of a pyrrhic victory. The following year, he commanded the rearguard of the French army as it retreated out of Portugal, fighting successful actions at Pombal, Redinha and Casal Novo and so stopping Wellington cutting off the main French army in Spain. However, Ney then fell out with Napoleon's brother, his nominal superior, and so was moved to join the invasion of Russia in 1812. It was during this campaign that he gained the nickname of 'Bravest of the Brave'. In 1814, he led the marshals who demanded Napoleon's abdication and then transferred his loyalties to the restored King Louis XVIII of France.

CHAPTER 4

'THE PRUSSIANS WERE VERY ROUGHLY HANDLED'

Wellington in a letter to Lady Frances Webster, 16 June 1815

Although the main focus of attention was in the Netherlands, the war had actually already started hundreds of kilometres away to the south. Acting without orders and entirely contrary to the agreed plan of campaign, the Austrian commander in northern Italy, General Frimont, had decided to invade France.

Frimont's move was unexpected, but it did make sense. He was concerned that Napoleon might decide to open the war with a lightning strike into Italy, and with good reason. Frimont's army had just fought the campaign against Murat in Naples. The men were tired, stocks of ammunition were low and units were scattered on garrison duty.

Frimont knew that secret pro-revolutionary societies were active in the large cities of northern Italy – Milan, Turin, Genoa, Venice and elsewhere. These societies had promised to rise in support of Murat when he arrived so long as he brought them weapons. Assuredly, they would rise if Napoleon entered Italy. If the reformists of the big Italian cities rose with success, it was likely that the revolutionaries of the larger German cities would do likewise. That would make the positions of the Austrian Schwarzenberg and the Russian Tolly difficult or even impossible if the armies of the smaller German states deserted the alliance.

A quick victory in northern Italy could be achieved and at little cost – and it might turn the entire tide of the war. Frimont was right to be worried.

Frimont had two objectives in moving forward. First he wanted to seize the mountain passes, which would be easier to defend than the open plains of northern Italy. Second, he determined to probe the French positions to get some idea of how strong the French armies in the area actually were.

Frimont split his army into two. The I Corps under Field Marshal Radivojevich was to advance into France over the mountains close to the Swiss frontier. The II Corps under Count Bubna was to advance over the Mount Cenis Pass further south. The advance began late on 14 June. At first the Austro-Italian army encountered no resistance. For the next five days, while the entire Waterloo campaign was being fought, Frimont's forces advanced slowly along the difficult roads to get into southern France.

News of Napoleon's move into the Netherlands reached Engelhardt and the German Corps on 16 June. Engelhardt got his men moving that afternoon, marching towards Arlon in the southern Netherlands. He was intending to threaten the right flank and rear of Napoleon's advancing army. This might disrupt the French supply lines, or might persuade Napoleon to detach units from his main army to block the German advance. In the event, Napoleon did not receive news of Engelhardt's advance until after the Battle of Waterloo was over.

British army in confusion

Back in the Netherlands, Wellington's army had been reduced to a state of utter confusion. Three sets of orders had been sent out between 5 pm and 2 am during the night. In most cases, units had received their first orders during the evening. These had instructed units to gather at a divisional meeting place overnight and to be ready to move at dawn. The second set of orders had told units to concentrate at Nivelles, or in some cases nearby. Most units had received these orders by the early hours of the morning, but some had not – since they had moved from their original locations in accordance with the first orders. The third orders had told all units to go to Quatre Bras as quickly as possible. Only a few units had received these orders by dawn since in most cases the messengers could not find them – either because they had moved, or because the messengers got lost in the dark or simply due to the confusion caused by so many units being on the move at once.

The result was that by dawn many units were without orders, many had not reached where they thought they were meant to be and others had no idea what they were supposed to be doing.

For instance, Captain Mercer of the Royal Horse Artillery had as his second set of orders to go to Braine-le-Comte and there to await Major MacDonald of the RHA, who would give him further orders when and if necessary. Mercer got to the rendezvous, though not without having lost his ammunition wagons. They turned up three hours later having taken a different road, but there was no sign of MacDonald. By lunchtime Mercer was still without orders, though thousands of men were streaming past him heading east. When he spotted General Vandeleur of the Dutch dragoons, Mercer rode over to ask advice. 'I know nothing about you, sir,' came the brusque reply and Vandeleur rode on.

At 3 pm another battery of the RHA came clattering by, led by Major Bull. Again Mercer asked advice. Bull said that Mercer should follow him, even though he had no orders either and was instead following a regiment of dragoons who did have firm orders. Mercer set off with his guns and an hour later was overtaken by the errant Major MacDonald who handed him orders to accompany the Household Brigade of cavalry. Unfortunately, neither Mercer nor MacDonald knew where the Household Brigade was, so Mercer carried on with Major Bull and the dragoons. He eventually ended up at Quatre Bras after nightfall.

The sheer scale of the confusion was not appreciated by

Wellington, nor by his staff led by de Lancey. The British army had standard tables that gave times that should be allowed for messengers to travel cross-country and deliver orders and for the unit receiving the orders to get underway. De Lancey applied these standardized times to the third set of orders and worked out where each unit should be. The vast majority of them were not there, of course. However, Wellington would base his actions that day on de Lancey's estimates.

Commanders at Brye
At about 10 am Wellington arrived at Quatre Bras to find the crossroads defended by some 8,000 men with more arriving by the minute. The French, he was told, had launched some small-scale probing attacks about two hours earlier but had been quiet since. Assuming all was well, Wellington rode on to the east to try to find Blücher. The two men and their staffs met at the windmill at Brye.

The following conversation was only slightly hindered by the fact that Wellington spoke no German while Blücher and Gneisenau spoke no English. Müffling acted as interpreter. When the pleasantries were over, Wellington asked a question that appeared to be simple, but was not. 'What do you want me to do?'

Blücher and Gneisenau knew exactly what they wanted Wellington to do and were delighted by his co-operative attitude. After all, they both had lingering doubts about British commitment to the cause and all three knew of the diplomatic disputes that had taken place in Vienna and that might break out again at any time.

Blücher's plan of campaign envisaged his army standing on the defensive at Ligny to halt the French advance, while Wellington marched from Quatre Bras to take the French in the left flank and ensure their destruction. It seemed a simple enough plan, but there were problems. For a start, Blücher had only part of his army with him at Ligny. The I Corps of Zieten was there, but had been disordered and weakened by its fighting retreat of the previous day. The II Corps of Georg von Pirch was present in full, as was von Thielmann's III Corps. However, Bülow's IV Corps was still miles away and was unlikely to arrive that day. Nevertheless, Blücher had 84,000 men at Ligny.

The second problem was not known to the commanders. De Lancey's estimates had it that Wellington's army would be concentrated at Quatre Bras by mid afternoon. Once gathered, they would then march to Ligny and arrive at perhaps 5 pm. In fact, the army was so scattered and disorganized that it would not reach Quatre Bras before nightfall.

Wellington turned to the map and pointed out his reservations about Blücher's plan. He indicated the two main roads to Brussels from Quatre Bras and Nivelles. By marching to Ligny, Wellington would be leaving these roads undefended. Napoleon was famous for his quick manoeuvring and might opt to change direction suddenly and march up one of these roads to seize Brussels. Wellington did not mention his secret orders to keep the line of retreat open to the Royal Navy in the Scheldt, but this was his real objection to leaving the roads unguarded.

Blücher and Gneisenau could not understand Wellington's objections, and said so. At this point Müffling reminded Wellington that the Netherlands army under the Prince of Orange was much closer to Quatre Bras than the British troops. Wellington nodded, concluding that he could send the Dutch to help the Prussians while keeping some of his British troops back to guard the retreat route to the Scheldt. He turned to Blücher, said he expected his army to be gathered at Quatre Bras by 4 pm and said, 'Well then, I will come – provided I

Opposite: As the Prussian army began to disintegrate in the later stages of the Battle of Ligny, Blücher was pinned to the ground by his dead horse while rival cavalry fought across him. He concealed his injuries to lead his reformed army back into action at Waterloo.

am not attacked myself.' With that, Wellington and Müffling mounted their horses and rode off, while Gneisenau and Blücher returned to Ligny to finish arranging their army for a defensive battle.

Deployments at Ligny

The position at Ligny was undoubtedly a strong one and well suited to defence. From where the French were, near Fleurus, the main road to Sombreffe and on to Gembloux and Germany appeared to run over a gently undulating plain. In fact, the plain was cut by the Ligny stream, which ran through a small, steep-sided valley. The stream itself was relatively small, but its banks were a tangle of woodlands with dense undergrowth that would be a real obstacle to any troops seeking to get through them. Along the stream were to be found the village of Ligny itself, plus the hamlets of Wagnelée, Saint-Amand-la-Haye, Saint-Amand, Tongrinelle, Boignée and Balâtre, plus a ruined castle and a handful of farms. All this was invisible to Napoleon.

In order to make the hidden stream even more of an obstacle, Blücher had his troops hack loopholes in any buildings facing the stream and build barricades where the stream's banks were not blocked by undergrowth. Into these defences Blücher put a force of infantry with some artillery support. Most of his army was positioned on the higher ground behind the valley so that troops could be moved down to support any threatened sector as the French attack developed. Expecting Wellington to arrive on his right flank in the later afternoon, Blücher had left that flank relatively weak.

It was these dispositions that Napoleon saw when he arrived at 11 am. Unaware of the fortified stream, he saw only the Prussian forces on the high ground and concluded that Blücher was in a weak position, especially on his right. Blücher would only adopt a position like this if he were expecting help from Wellington, but it did lay his army open to utter defeat if it were attacked before Wellington arrived.

Napoleon quickly issued his orders. Ney was to block the road from Nivelles to Ligny at Quatre Bras to stop Wellington from reaching the Prussians. He was to do this with Reille's II Corps and Kellerman's heavy cavalry. D'Erlon's I Corps was to stand behind Ney to act as a mobile reserve able to go to help Ney or Napoleon as circumstances demanded. D'Erlon was, however, some miles to the south and it would take hours for him to come up.

Meanwhile, Napoleon and Grouchy would attack the Prussians at Ligny with Grouchy's command of the III Corps under Vandamme, the IV Corps under Gérard plus the I, II and IV Cavalry Corps. Napoleon's central reserve of Lobau's VI Corps and the Imperial Guard would also move on Ligny, though like d'Erlon they would take some time to arrive. His plan was to engage the Prussians all along their front to probe for a weak point. Having found one, he would then launch a massed attack to smash the weak point and burst through the Prussian army and destroy it.

French launch assault
Napoleon waited until he heard a distant rumble of cannon coming from the north-west at a little after 2 pm. That signalled that Ney was in action at Quatre Bras and was blocking Wellington's advance to Ligny. Confident that his left was now secure, Napoleon sent Vandamme and Gérard forward with their corps to begin assaults on the Prussian army. It was only at this point that the French discovered the Ligny stream and the way the Prussians had fortified both it and the hamlets along its length. For the next hour or more the French probed forward, but found themselves confronted by a well positioned enemy and made little progress despite taking heavy casualties.

At 3.30 pm, realizing that the task ahead of him was tougher than he had thought, Napoleon sent Count de la Bédoyère to find Ney and order him to send d'Erlon's I Corps down the main Nivelles–Sombreffe road. This would bring d'Erlon and his 21,000 men on to the right rear flank of the Prussians near Wagnelée. From there d'Erlon would be able to roll up the Prussian army. Combined with a frontal assault by Napoleon this would trap the Prussian army and destroy it utterly. Rapid calculations told Napoleon that d'Erlon would arrive at about 6 pm.

At 4 pm, Napoleon concentrated his 12-pounder guns in front of Ligny itself and unleashed a heavy bombardment on the village. Before long the village was a mass of burning rubble. Gérard sent his infantry in and drove the Prussians out of the southern half of the village. But before Gérard's men could get over the bridge to take the rest of the village, Blücher sent in heavy reinforcements. The two sides found themselves facing each other over the narrow stream, firing from crumbling houses, many of which were on fire. Casualties began to mount alarmingly on both sides as the murderous struggle dragged on beyond 5 pm.

The fighting on both flanks had been less intense, but just as inconclusive. The French had captured Saint-Amand-la-Haye, Boignée and Tongrinelle but were unable to get over the stream in any real strength.

Blücher believed that the battle was going well. He was holding the French attack all along the line and it was approaching the time when he was expecting Wellington's advance units to arrive. He began mustering his reserves to deliver an attack on his right wing. This, he hoped, would turn the French left wing and drive them west towards Wellington's advancing army. The Prussian hammer would smash the French army against Wellington's anvil.

Napoleon, meanwhile, was expecting d'Erlon to arrive. He, too, was mustering forces for a major offensive. He hoped to smash through the Prussian centre, crush the Prussian right between his own troops and those of d'Erlon, then drive the surviving Prussians off towards Germany. That would leave Wellington isolated and vulnerable.

The approach of d'Erlon

At 5.30 pm both French and Prussian scouting cavalry out beyond the western edge of the battlefield sighted large columns of infantry accompanied by cavalry marching towards Ligny. The columns were coming from the direction of Frasnes, just south of Quatre Bras, and were heading towards Wagnelée so as to arrive on the French left flank from behind. The French scouts identified the distant columns as being Dutch and numbering around 20,000 men. The Prussian scouts also counted 20,000 men but identified them as being French.

This confusion as to who was marching toward Ligny was understandable. Although states dressed their armies in brightly coloured uniforms to make identification easier, the Dutch army had until a few months earlier been allied to the French. They wore short, dark-blue jackets with grey trousers and a shako hat that was more or less cylindrical, but higher at the front than the back. The French wore a long, dark-blue jacket with buff trousers and a shako that was wider at the top than the bottom. At close quarters the uniforms were easy to tell apart by the detailing, but at a distance one dark-blue jacket could easily be mistaken for the other.

Vandamme, commanding the III Corps on the French left, was first to receive the reports of the advancing Dutch force. He called off his attack on the Prussians, pulling one division out of the line and turning them to face west to meet the expected attack. Vandamme did some quick calculations regarding his own and the opposing forces and then sent a message to Napoleon saying that, unless reinforcements were forthcoming, he would be forced to pull back as soon as the Dutch attack began.

Napoleon received the reports of the approaching Dutch at a little after 5.30 pm, together with Vandamme's request for reinforcements. He responded by calling off his planned attack on the Prussian centre. He then moved two divisions of the Guard toward his left, ready to support Vandamme if they were needed. Napoleon was, however, puzzled. According to the latest information that he had, the Dutch should be engaged fighting Ney at Quatre Bras. He sent his own scouts to reconnoitre the approaching column and to report as soon as possible.

Gneisenau and Blücher had by this time also received reports that a French army was approaching. From where they stood on high ground behind the Prussian army they could not see the advancing troops. They could, however, see Vandamme move troops out of the attack to face west. They concluded that the approaching troops must be those of Wellington, not French after all. Vandamme was a lot closer to the oncoming army than they were and they thought that he was in a better position to identify them.

When Blücher saw Napoleon move divisions of his Imperial Guard to face west and move toward Vandamme, it convinced him that Wellington was approaching in force. He gave orders that the Prussian attack was to go ahead at once.

As the Prussians were gathering for the assault, Napoleon's personal scouts came back to report that the approaching troops were, in fact, those of d'Erlon.

Napoleon was both relieved and annoyed – relieved to find the new arrivals were French, not Dutch, but annoyed that d'Erlon was arriving on the French flank not on that of the Prussians. D'Erlon's attack would therefore be less destructive than Napoleon had hoped, but nonetheless useful. He sent orders to d'Erlon to veer to his left, so heading more directly toward the Prussians. Napoleon then began moving his Imperial Guard back into position to launch his planned assault.

Mass attacks

Suddenly, at 6 pm, the Prussian attack surged forward. Leading the way were heavy cavalry, supported by dense columns of infantry and horse artillery. They surged over the stream and into the French positions held by Vandamme. Vandamme was caught reorganizing his defences – having realized it was d'Erlon, not Wellington, coming up on his left. The Prussians, expecting the French to be trapped between two fires, attacked with reckless courage. Vandamme's men were pushed back and for a while it looked as if they were about to break. Then Vandamme got his reserve division into action and the Prussian attack ground to a halt.

A little after 7.30 pm, Napoleon unleashed his own mass attack. He moved his artillery to face the Prussian centre and opened up a furious barrage that inflicted heavy casualties. As the cannon pounded away, Napoleon formed up two massive attack columns, both spearheaded by the Imperial Guard and supported by dense masses of heavy cavalry. The French guns fell silent to avoid hitting their own men just as the columns reached the Prussian lines. With barely a delay, the French Imperial Guard smashed its way through the first line of Prussian defences and began to mount the slope beyond. Blücher had no reserves left and it was clear that the few Prussian infantry on the crest of the hill would break and run as soon as the Imperial Guard reached them.

Prussians forced back

Gneisenau and Blücher were appalled. They could not understand how Napoleon could be launching an attack when, as they thought, Wellington was assaulting his left flank. While Gneisenau sent off desperate messages to the commanders on the flank to tell them of the dire situation, Blücher leapt on his horse and spurred off to a nearby regiment of hussars. Despite his 72 years, Blücher was an energetic man. He paused only long enough to send off messengers with orders to bring every cavalry unit to the spot. Then he led the hussars in a charge at the advancing French columns.

The French calmly formed square to receive cavalry, then

delivered a devastating volley of musket fire that emptied many Prussian saddles. The hussars fell back. They had, however, forced the French infantry to deploy from column into square. It is much more difficult to march a regiment over fields in square than in column, so the French advance was slowed considerably.

Returning to his start position, Blücher found more cavalry had answered his summons. Issuing orders to some infantry who had also come to his aid, Blücher led yet another reckless cavalry charge at the advancing French columns. The infantry that he had left behind formed themselves into an ad hoc rearguard behind which the more disorganized units could fall back to get away from the French. Meanwhile, Gneisenau's messages had reached the Prussian wings and they, too, began to retreat.

Gneisenau, at about this time, received word from his scouts that the large marching columns that had been approaching from the west had vanished. Nobody could say for certain where they had gone. While attention had been focused on events on the battlefields the thousands of men had vanished like smoke in the wind.

To make matters even worse, Blücher had vanished as well. He had last been seen leading a cavalry charge at Napoleon's Imperial Guard, which was flanked by a squadron of heavy cuirassier cavalry. He had not been seen since, and Gneisenau had to assume that his commander was dead.

Gneisenau was both worried and furious. He was worried for his army and furious with Wellington for having apparently abandoned the Prussian army in its hour of need and fled for the safety of the Royal Navy. He quickly reviewed the situation. The Prussians had started the day with about 80,000 men. Around 10,000 of them were now dead, another 30,000 or so were streaming to the rear having lost all formation and discipline. That left around 40,000 men who were still in their units, but who had in the main lost cohesion and morale and who had suffered casualties, some units heavily. The centre of the army was smashed to pieces and the two wings were retreating hastily and without contact with each other, and Blücher was missing. To his front was Napoleon with the entire French army. Somewhere to the west, Wellington was apparently fleeing for safety.

The only realistic option that Gneisenau could see was to fall back on Bülow's advancing and intact IV Corps. Once a junction with Bülow had been effected the Prussian army would retreat to Germany to await political developments. Looking at his map and estimating where Bülow would be, Gneisenau set Tilly as the rendezvous point and began issuing orders to the officers of the retreating army to muster there at first light. A staff officer, von Reiche, referred to the standard map that had been issued to regimental officers and realized that Tilly was not marked on it. The next place along the road that led through Tilly and was marked on all maps was Wavre. He suggested that Gneisenau give orders to muster at Wavre at noon, instead of Tilly at dawn. On such small incidents do the fates of nations turn.

Into the gathering darkness streamed the defeated Prussian army.

Victory within reach
Napoleon, meanwhile, was just as furious as was Gneisenau. He did at least know that the advancing columns had been those of d'Erlon's corps, but he no more knew where they had gone than did the Prussians. With the Prussian centre having been smashed by the Imperial Guard and the two wings retreating in different directions, now was the time for the enemy army to be ripped to pieces and destroyed as a fighting force. All that was needed was for d'Erlon and his fresh men to surge forward and fall on the Prussian flank and rear. But where was d'Erlon? He and his men had apparently vanished off the face of the Earth.

August von Gneisenau

Born in 1760 into a family of minor Saxon nobility that had fallen on hard times, Gneisenau used family contacts to get a job as an officer in the army of one of Germany's many small states, Bayreuth-Ansbach. The Prince of Ansbach was seriously in debt, and sought to earn income by renting his army out to the highest bidder. Gneisenau therefore found himself fighting alongside the British army in the American War of Independence. It was there that he gained important experience both of the conventional British forces and of the light infantry tactics espoused by the Americans. The prince finally solved his financial problems by selling sovereignty over his state to King Frederick Wilhelm II of Prussia, and so Gneisenau passed into Prussian service.

As a Prussian officer, Gneisenau spent a lot of time on academic military research and on perfecting his skills as a staff administrative officer. In 1806, he was commanding the small fortress of Kolberg on the Baltic coast. His defence against French besiegers proved to be a masterclass and established his reputation as a fighting officer. After Prussia's defeat by France, Gneisenau played a key role in reforming the Prussian army as a fully modern, effective fighting force. In 1812, when Prussia went to war with France again, he was appointed as Chief of Staff to Blücher and was still holding that post in 1815. The two men formed an effective partnership with Gneisenau's careful staff work forming the perfect complement to Blucher's aggressive and dashing grasp of strategic possiblities. He later served as Governor of Berlin and was showered with honours. Through careful management of his pay and other rewards, he managed to rebuild his family's fortunes and he bought sizeable estates in Silesia. He died of cholera in 1831.

By 10 pm it was clear to Napoleon that he had had the Prussian army at his mercy, but that somehow they had slipped away. Leaving orders for his army to regroup around Ligny and for scouts to ride out to find where the various units of the Prussian army were going, Napoleon rode back to his headquarters at Fleurus for supper, bed and some serious thinking.

CHAPTER 5

'IF WE CANNOT STOP HIM THERE ...'

Wellington in a letter to Lady Frances Webster, 16 June 1815

After his meeting with Blücher, Wellington rode back to Quatre Bras to await the arrival of his army. Almost as soon as he got there he realized that something was wrong. He had been expecting to find a sizeable portion of his army already gathered around the crossroads, with more arriving every minute. Instead, by 2 pm there was still only the Prince of Orange with 8,000 men and 16 cannon of the Netherlands army.

In some desperation, Wellington sent riders out to try to find his army and get it to march to Quatre Bras. He soon had other matters on his mind.

French attack at Quatre Bras
At 2 pm a shattering roar signalled the start of a heavy cannonade from the French lines. Ney had been mustering Reille's II Corps all morning. His orders from Napoleon had been both precise and maddeningly vague. Ney had been told to 'hold the crossroads at Quatre Bras in strength' to stop Wellington's army marching to aid Blücher at Ligny – this despite the fact that the crossroads were actually held by Wellington, not Ney. He was also ordered 'to support with every man at his disposal' Napoleon's attack on the Prussians. How Ney was supposed to hold a crossroads he did not hold and at the same time send his command to support Napoleon was not made clear. Napoleon was clearly missing the skills

of his deceased chief of staff, Berthier. Ney decided that his first priority had to be to capture the crossroads.

Ney rode up the main road to view the situation for himself. At 1.30 pm he found that the crossroads was held by relatively few men. Two farms – Pierrepont and Gemioncourt – stood about 1,000 m south of the crossroads and were held by Dutch infantry with artillery behind them. To the west was a large wood with dense undergrowth, the Bois de Bossu.

Ney quickly realized that he could not attack the crossroads until the Bois de Bossu was secured. He told Reille to send his light infantry into the wood at once. Reille hesitated. 'This may turn out to be like in Spain when you don't see the British until they attack you.' Reille was referring to Wellington's habit of positioning his troops on the reverse sides of hills, behind woods or other places where they were out of shot of the French artillery, and out of sight of the French commanders, until he needed them. Ney, who like Reille had fought Wellington in Spain, delayed his assault until all of Reille's corps had arrived.

Ney decided to try to obey his contradictory orders by dividing his force. He brought Reille's II Corps up to attack Quatre Bras. D'Erlon's I Corps was behind Reille on the road north from Charleroi. Ney sent him orders that he was to continue north to Frasnes, then halt there to await orders. This would put d'Erlon in a position to continue north to support Ney, or turn east along another main road to support Napoleon.

As his guns roared out, Ney sent infantry forward to take the farms south of Quatre Bras. The fighting was intense, but within 45 minutes both farms had fallen. Ney then pushed light infantry into the Bois de Bossu on his left while forming up men on the right to assault the Dutch holding the main road east of the crossroads. Rather ironically, these units were commanded by Colonel Westenberg, Commander of the Dutch Royal Guard who had until a year earlier commanded a battalion in Napoleon's Imperial Guard.

British reinforcements

As the French formed up to advance, a column of British redcoat infantry came into sight marching south along the main road from Brussels. These were the lead units of the British 5th Division, under Lieutenant General Thomas Picton. They had been camping around Brussels and so had avoided the confusion engulfing nearly every other British unit. Welcome as they were, the advancing British regiments were strung out along the road in the order they had left Brussels. They would be arriving piecemeal in no coherent order over a period of two or three hours. It is an indication of Wellington's priorities that the first battalion to arrive was sent to the east to hold the road leading to Ligny and secure the route Wellington hoped to take as soon as his main army turned up. When the 28th Regiment arrived, it was sent to help the garrison of Gemioncourt, but seeing that farm in French hands, they turned around and fell back on the crossroads. As they fell back, a force of dragoons in green galloped up shouting in French. Assuming the dragoons were French, who wore green, the redcoats opened fire and killed many horses and a few men. In fact the cavalry were Dutch dragoons. Once again the similarities between Dutch and French uniforms were having tragic results.

At about 4 pm, Duke Frederick William of Brunswick arrived with his army, officially part of Wellington's 6th Division under General Sir Lowry Cole. Brunswick was another of the small independent states of Germany and its army numbered some 5,000 men and was made up of line infantry, light infantry, guard infantry and the ducal artillery plus small numbers of lancer and hussar cavalry. Wellington asked Brunswick to take his small army to the right of the crossroads to drive back French skirmishers working north along the edge of the Bois de Bossu.

Infantry squares

By 5 pm, the French had control of the Bois de Bossu while Picton's men were engaged in a musketry duel at close quarters with Reille's infantry advancing on the crossroads. Ney now pushed forward his heavy cavalry and lancers, which forced Picton's redcoats and Brunswick's black-clad men to form square. These dense formations were proof against cavalry, but with the men so tightly packed they were highly vulnerable to artillery. When a battery of French horse artillery opened fire at close range it began to inflict high casualties.

The Duke of Brunswick was hit by a musket ball and thrown from his horse as the French cavalry moved forward – apparently to charge his infantry. Getting the Brunswick infantry into square when they had just seen their beloved duke mortally wounded was a struggle and they only just made it in time. Seeing the infantry well formed, the cuirassiers pulled back. The French artillery was not so considerate and – although at long range – was deadly accurate.

Wellington ordered his infantry to fall back behind the crossroads to get out of range of the French cannon. Ney chose this moment to hurl his heavy cavalry and lancers forward in a smashing charge. Wellington himself was caught in the open as a squadron of cuirassiers emerged from the smoke. He had to jump his horse over the heads of the infantry of the 92nd Highlanders, shouting at them to duck, to gain the safety of their square. Regiments of Dutch and Hanoverian infantry were caught out of square and were butchered by the French cavalry.

Watching the unfolding confusion in Wellington's centre, Ney was jubilant. He could see that only a part of Wellington's army had arrived and that the rest was turning up in some confusion. He guessed, correctly, that most of Wellington's army was strung out on the roads south of Brussels in confusion and disorder. Now he had broken through Wellington's position at Quatre Bras. The road to Brussels was open and with it the

Opposite: An illustration showing the advance of the British redcoats on the French in blue that took place in the evening of 16 June at Quatre Bras. The battle ended in something of a stalemate, though the British had possession of the field.

opportunity to smash Wellington's army bit by bit with ease.

Ney sent an urgent message to d'Erlon waiting at Frasnes to hurry forward and join the victorious pursuit of Wellington's broken army. But d'Erlon and his 20,000 men had gone. Ney was astounded. Where on earth was d'Erlon?

Without d'Erlon's fresh men, Ney had to spend some time reorganizing his own forces to exploit his success. By that time, Wellington had been reinforced by the British 3rd Division under Sir Charles Alten. As the red-coated infantry moved forward to bolster the defensive positions, Wellington became rather more confident that he could hold Quatre Bras. He still had very few cavalry and almost no infantry, but his fresh British infantry should have been able to hold off the French forces he could see ranged against him. The problem would come if Ney were to be reinforced.

Napoleon's call for help

Ney, meanwhile, had just received a message from Napoleon written by Soult, telling him about the battle raging around Ligny. The message continued, 'His Majesty desires me to tell you that you are to manoeuvre immediately in such a manner as to envelop the enemy's right and fall upon his rear – the army in our front is lost if you act with energy. THE FATE OF FRANCE IS IN YOUR HANDS. Do not hesitate for a moment.'

Ney was exasperated. If he sought to disengage from Wellington, he would be presenting the rear of his battered divisions to the fresh men that were joining Wellington. A disaster was more than possible. And anyway, where was d'Erlon? He scanned the battlefield, only to see the Hanoverian army arriving to bolster Wellington. Once again, he sent out messengers to try to find d'Erlon and bring him up to Quatre Bras before Wellington gained the upper hand and was able to slip around Ney's flank to join Blücher.

Wellington chose this moment to push his infantry forward in an effort to retake the farms. The British infantry were advancing through fields of rye standing some 2 m tall. This meant that Ney could see only swaying rye and could not be certain how many infantry were on the move. It also meant that the infantry could not see the trap Ney was preparing for them. He was sending forward 1,000 cuirassiers, backed by 800 lighter cavalry and as many infantry as were in good order to advance.

The Prince of Orange had ordered the British infantry to advance in line so that they could bring their massed musket fire to bear on the French infantry he had seen beyond the rye. The British officers, alerted by the sounds of thundering hooves, gave the order to get into square, but for the 69th and 73rd regiments it was too late. The cuirassiers were on them before they could get into square. The slaughter was horrific as the scattered infantry fell easy prey to the big horsemen. The King's Colour of the 69th was captured, a humiliating blow to the regimental pride. Both regiments fled back for the safety of the hedged roads around the crossroads, followed by the 33rd when it came under heavy artillery fire. The remaining infantry in squares among the rye came under attack at the hands of the light cavalry, but managed to hold their own. The cuirassiers swept on until they met the steady Brunswickers lining the hedges, supported by artillery.

It was now 6.30 pm, and Wellington was deeply relieved to see General Sir George Cooke arrive with four battalions of the British Guards. Wellington sent them to his right to support Picton's battered men. He resumed his advance, but Ney blocked the advance with infantry and artillery acting in close unison. At around 9 pm the light began to go as the sun sank, and gradually the fighting around Quatre Bras came to an end. Ney decided to withdraw back towards Frasnes to reorganize Reille's corps. He left behind a rearguard to watch Wellington. Ney was reasonably content with how the day had gone, though the sudden disappearance of d'Erlon had robbed him of a complete victory over Wellington. Still he had stopped Wellington going to Ligny, which had been his primary objective.

Wellington, however, was less pleased. He had promised Blücher that he would arrive at Ligny by late afternoon, and he had failed to do so. He was also painfully aware that his army was spread across a large area of ground, was confused and muddled. Even at this late stage, Wellington could not be certain where much of his army was nor whether it had received his orders to come to Quatre Bras. Once again, messengers were sent out to find the lost units and bring them to Wellington at Quatre Bras.

D'Erlon's movements – a missed opportunity
Jean-Baptiste Drouet, Count d'Erlon, had been having an extremely trying day. He had woken at dawn at Jumet, just north of Charleroi. With him he had two of his four divisions, the other two having been held up trying to get over the narrow bridges over the Sambre. He had in his hands Ney's orders from the previous evening that he was to concentrate his corps into a compact body as the enemy were only a few kilometres north. D'Erlon therefore waited for his two rear divisions to come up before starting the march north up the main road to Quatre Bras and Brussels.

He had reached Gosselies when his cavalry scouts out to the west sent in an urgent message that large columns of the enemy were approaching. D'Erlon at once halted his advance and began deploying his corps to give battle. The columns turned out to be elements of Wellington's scattered army heading for Quatre Bras. They ignored the French cavalry scouts and were unaware of d'Erlon's presence. Once this was established, d'Erlon continued his march north. At this point he received Ney's order to halt at Frasnes and await further orders. D'Erlon and his

Opposite: The French cuirassiers catch the British 69th and 73rd Regiments in line. The British did not have time to form a defensive square and suffered heavy casualties.

forward units reached Frasnes, where a temporary headquarters was established. D'Erlon then rode back to hurry up his rear units. At about 3.30 pm Napoleon's personal ADC, Charles de la Bédoyère, arrived in Frasnes with an order to d'Erlon from Napoleon. De la Bédoyère used his position to 'speak as if he were the emperor'. In the absence of d'Erlon he gave his message to General Delcambre, d'Erlon's Chief of Staff. The orders were to march on Ligny and Saint-Amand to attack the Prussians, with whom Napoleon was engaged in battle. Delcambre turned to his subordinate, General de Salle, and ordered him to get the corps moving in accordance with Napoleon's instructions. He then rode off to find d'Erlon, while de la Bédoyère rode back to Napoleon. As the units of I Corps came up to Frasnes, de Salle turned them east towards Ligny. Delcambre found d'Erlon, who then galloped off to get to the head of his corps as it marched on Ligny.

By 5.30 pm he was approaching Ligny, and it was at this point that he and his men were spotted by French and Prussian cavalry scouts. Those sightings precipitated the final moves at Ligny that led to the Prussian defeat. At 6 pm, however, Ney's order to d'Erlon instructing him to come to Quatre Bras finally caught up with the commander of I Corps. He now had totally contradictory orders. Ney wanted him at Quatre Bras, Napoleon wanted him at Ligny. The standard procedures of the French army were quite clear about how an officer should behave in such circumstances. An officer had a duty to obey his immediate superior (Ney) unless a more senior commander (Napoleon) were actually on the spot and issuing orders.

D'Erlon compared the two sets of orders. Napoleon's gave the impression that the battle at Ligny was going well and that d'Erlon was only desired to come and help out. Ney's letter emphasized the urgency of the situation and made it clear that d'Erlon was needed. All things considered, d'Erlon decided that he had no choice but to obey Ney. Nevertheless, two of his divisions were almost at Ligny so he ordered them to continue in order to join Napoleon. The rest of his column was to turn around and go back to Quatre Bras.

D'Erlon spurred back down his column to take personal charge of his rearguard, now his advance guard. The process of turning 20,000 men around was slow and inevitably led to some confusion, but even so d'Erlon got his men underway with commendable speed.

The two divisions that d'Erlon sent to help Napoleon advanced until they ran into Prussian troops near Wagnelée. Entirely ignorant of how the battle was going, they then halted and messengers were sent to try to find Napoleon and ask for orders. This had the unfortunate effect of giving the Prussian right wing time to get away before the divisions were ordered to attack what had been, when they first arrived, the isolated and disorganized Prussian divisions to their front.

D'Erlon got back to Frasnes at 8 pm to find urgent messages from Ney wanting to know where he was and what he was doing. D'Erlon led his forward units up the road toward Quatre Bras just in time to meet Ney falling back to regroup. A remarkably amicable discussion – given the circumstances – then followed. D'Erlon then pushed some of his units up to Quatre Bras to take over the duties of rearguard from Reille's men, who needed supper and sleep. D'Erlon must have realized that if he had been at either Quatre Bras or Ligny he would have been instrumental in winning a great victory for Napoleon. As it was he had been at neither and no victory had been won.

At the end of the day

Night finally fell on 16 June with Wellington wondering how the Prussians had fared, Gneisenau falling back north before retreating home to Germany without Blücher who was presumed dead, Ney wondering how Napoleon had got on but confident he would attack Wellington next morning with d'Erlon's men and Napoleon hopping mad with d'Erlon and puzzled as to where the Prussians had gone. The campaign was still undecided despite the thousands of men who had died.

COMTE D'ERLON

Jean-Baptiste Drouet, Comte d'Erlon, was born into humble circumstances in Reims in 1765. He joined the French army and had worked his way up to the rank of corporal when the Revolution began. In 1793 his fellow soldiers elected him captain of the company and from there he was promoted to the rank of general, by 1799. He fought across Germany, Switzerland and Poland in the years that followed, but his fame was established in Spain. In 1810 he managed to defeat a British army under Viscount Hill, going on to achieve a string of impressive if small-scale successes against Spanish and Portuguese forces. When Napoleon abdicated in 1814, d'Erlon transferred his loyalty to Louis XVIII, but then rushed to join Napoleon in 1815. After Napoleon abdicated a second time, he fled to live with friends in Bavaria. It was not until 1825 that he was given a pardon and allowed to return to France. In 1830, he rejoined the French army, serving until his death in 1844.

CHAPTER 6

'WITH YOUR SWORD IN HIS BACK'

Napoleon's verbal order to Grouchy about pursuing Blücher, 17 June 1815

A little after midnight the Prussian Chief of Staff and temporary commander, Gneisenau, was at Mellery just north of Tilly. He was waiting for reports to come in to confirm that his scattered army had got his orders to converge on Wavre. He was also waiting for Bülow of the IV Corps to arrive. That prickly nobleman and veteran soldier outranked Gneisenau and would, presumably, be taking command of the entire Prussian army when he arrived.

It was with enormous relief that Gneisenau saw a group of dragoons arrive, supporting among them the bruised, battered, but very much alive, figure of Blücher.

While leading the charge of Prussian cavalry at the French infantry, Blücher had had his horse shot dead from under him. When the horse collapsed, Blücher was thrown into the mud, his leg entangled in the stirrup leathers. The French cuirassiers then charged over him. Either they did not see him or thought he was dead because they made no effort to attack him. A few minutes later he was charged over again as the French cavalry retreated before a unit of Prussian cavalry. After the Prussians then charged over the stricken field marshal, also without taking any notice of him, Blücher finally managed to get free of his dead horse and clamber to his feet, which is when he was spotted by the Prussian dragoons and rescued.

Blücher, Gneisenau and half a dozen staff officers went into a barn and sat on barrels of pickled cabbage to decide their next moves. Gneisenau, still smarting from what he saw as Wellington's betrayal, wanted to retreat to Germany at once. Blücher wanted to stay close to Brussels so that he could co-operate with Wellington. That move was fraught with danger, because if Wellington was retreating in order to be evacuated by the Royal Navy the Prussians would have to face Napoleon alone. Blücher angrily ended the debate by saying, 'I have given my word, which is my sword, and I am too old to break it.'

It was decided that the army would continue to fall back on Wavre while scouts went out to try to locate both Wellington and the French. A final decision would be made at Wavre. Blücher then went off to have his bruises bathed in brandy – and to drink a fair amount of it, as well.

Dawn at Quatre Bras

Wellington slept the night in an inn at Genappe, a few miles north of Quatre Bras, but was up early the next day and arrived at Quatre Bras at dawn. He found that still only about half his army had arrived, and those men were cooking breakfast. He did, at least, know where the rest of it was. The units were strung out along the road running west from Quatre Bras to Nivelles. Both Quatre Bras and Nivelles were linked to Brussels by roads that converged at the hamlet of Mont-Saint-Jean, just south of Waterloo, a few kilometres north.

Looking south, Wellington could see the French forces of Ney arranged in some depth. He calculated that Ney had about the same number of men as himself, though with more artillery. It was clear to him that his position was exposed and vulnerable. If the Prussians had halted Napoleon at Ligny, then he and Blücher could still co-operate, but if Napoleon had broken through then Wellington might easily find himself outflanked.

Opposite: Napoleon surveys the positioning of Wellington's army on the morning of 18 June as he seeks to determine his plan of attack. On the day of the battle he rode the mare Desirée as his favoured stallion Marengo was tired after the previous two days.

By Permission of the Berlin Photographic Co., Bond Street, W.

NAPOLEON ON THE FIELD OF WATERLOO.

From the Painting by L. Royer.

Müffling had already sent riders east to try to locate Blücher and find out what was happening. At 6 am Wellington sent his own man, Colonel Alexander Gordon, with a troop of the elite 10th Light Dragoons. Wellington did not want to make a move until he knew what the Prussians were doing, but nor did he want to hang around at Quatre Bras longer than was necessary.

Ney, too, was at Quatre Bras by dawn, scanning Wellington's position. He knew that Napoleon had driven the Prussians out of Ligny, but without securing a total victory. At 6.30 am he sent a message to Napoleon telling him that Wellington was at Quatre Bras with about 25,000 men (in fact he had 40,000), with the rest of his army dispersed around the countryside south of Brussels. If Napoleon could send one corps, or preferably more, to attack the British from their left-rear the British army would be destroyed. Ney promised to attack Wellington with his entire force as soon as he heard Napoleon's guns.

At 8.30 am he received a message from Napoleon, written before Ney's message had arrived. After giving a brief overview of the fighting at Ligny, the message continued, 'The emperor is proceeding by the Quatre Bras Road to engage the enemy in front of you, whilst you attack them from in front with your divisions.' This was almost exactly what Ney had suggested. The key difference was that Napoleon had decided to wait until he heard Ney's guns before advancing. But Soult had not put that critical piece of evidence into his orders to Ney. So Ney waited until he heard Napoleon's guns, and Napoleon waited until he heard Ney's. Once again, the lack of Berthier was hampering Napoleon's action.

Napoleon orders pursuit of Blücher

Meanwhile, reports from French cavalry scouts came in regarding the movements of the Prussians. The reports were confusing and contradictory. One force of 6,000 Prussians was reported going south-east to Namur, another 5,000 were going north-east to Gembloux, 20,000 were going north to Wavre and a dozen other roads were clogged with stragglers, wounded and supply carts. Not until noon did it become clear to Napoleon that the bulk of the Prussian army was retiring toward Wavre. This was bad news, for it meant that Blücher would be able to co-operate with Wellington once his army had recovered from the mauling it had received at Ligny. On the other hand, the Prussian army would be unable to fight on this day, nor probably on the next. That gave Napoleon two days to deal with Wellington.

To make sure that Blücher could not interfere in his plans to deal with Wellington, Napoleon decided to detach Grouchy to pursue the Prussians and stop them from joining Wellington. Napoleon gave to Grouchy command of Vandamme's III Corps and Gérard's IV Corps plus the light cavalry of Pajol and heavy cavalry of Exelmans. Napoleon told Grouchy to chase Blücher 'with your sword in his back'.

Soult put Napoleon's orders into writing and sent these on after Grouchy later. These differed slightly from the verbal orders, telling Grouchy also to 'reconnoitre the roads towards Namur and Maastricht', to summon the National Guard from Charlemont to occupy Namur and a number of other tasks. The final instruction told Grouchy to maintain contact with Napoleon by way of cavalry units. This was quite a lot for Grouchy to do, in addition to keeping his sword in Blücher's back. Undoubtedly, these extra tasks slowed his pursuit of the Prussians.

At noon it occurred to Napoleon that he had not yet heard Ney's guns from Quatre Bras. He sent a terse order to Ney telling him to get on with attacking Wellington at once.

Wellington's planned retreat

But Wellington was no longer there to be attacked. One of Müffling's couriers had found Blücher on the road to Wavre. For the first time Blücher and Gneisenau learned that Wellington had been busy fighting Ney all the previous day and that the troops they had seen had been French, not Dutch. Reappraising his view of Wellington, Gneisenau now agreed with Blücher that the Prussians should co-operate with them. Until he had a better idea of the state of the Prussian army and what Napoleon was doing, Blücher was not able to give Wellington any sort of firm commitment as to what he would do, but he was definite that if Wellington stood and fought, so would he.

As soon as the news that the Prussians were going to Ligny reached Wellington he made a decision. He was going to retreat and fight Napoleon on ground of his own choosing. A year earlier, Wellington had ridden to Paris from Brussels using the very same road through Quatre Bras that he was now defending. During that ride he had passed the time by analysing the ground for its military potential. He had noted that there was a ridge south of Waterloo at Mont-Saint-Jean that would be easy to defend. It was at Mont-Saint-Jean that the roads from Nivelles and Quatre Bras joined. Moreover, a road heading north-west to Hal gave a good escape route to the Scheldt and the Royal Navy. Wellington therefore decided to hold Napoleon at Mont-Saint-Jean.

He sent orders that those units not yet at Quatre Bras should march north along the Nivelles–Brussels road to reach Mont-Saint-Jean. Those units at Quatre Bras would fall back directly north to the rendezvous. Wellington guessed that Napoleon would try to crush his army while the Prussians were still reeling from defeat at Ligny. He also guessed that Napoleon would be desperate for a quick victory and so would not try any clever, large-scale manoeuvres as he had done at Ulm in 1805. By blocking the road to Brussels just south of Waterloo, Wellington was making a large battle inevitable.

Opposite: A troop of horse artillery in their distinctive helmets pass Wellington who salutes them as they go by. The heavy rain on 17 June meant that artillery and heavy wagons had to stay on the paved main road, shown here, while the infantry and cavalry slogged through the mud.

Wellington sent a short note to Blücher outlining his intended actions and concluding, 'I will give Napoleon battle if I may hope to be supported by a single Prussian corps. But if this support is denied me, I shall be compelled to sacrifice Brussels and take up position behind the Scheldt.' Wellington still could not reveal his secret orders to Blücher, but went as far as he dared in warning the Prussians that if he did not receive their help he would be off. At 10 am Wellington began to retreat from Quatre Bras. He began by moving off those units that were not within sight of the French, hiding his retreat from them for as long as he could. The retreat was complicated by the large numbers of supply wagons that had been coming south from Brussels and which now needed to be turned around, but nonetheless it was got underway and by 12 noon units visible to the French began to move.

Ney saw them go and soon afterwards received the message from Napoleon telling him to get a move on. As he was starting to get his men moving, Napoleon arrived, attacking from the east into Wellington's rearguard commanded by Lord Uxbridge.

Almost at once, Napoleon's cavalry captured a man who had been making a tidy sum selling baked goods to the English and Dutch soldiers. Dragged in front of the emperor, the man was overawed and gabbled out that the British army had gone. Napoleon pointed to Uxbridge's force and demanded to know who they were then. The man replied that they were only a thin screen of troops, all the rest had marched north earlier.

Leaping on his horse, Napoleon led forward his cavalry and horse artillery, leaving Soult behind to bring up the infantry as fast as he could. It was 2 pm when he came within sight of the Quatre Bras crossroads. Wellington was on a hill to the north with Lord Uxbridge. For the first time Wellington saw Napoleon, though Napoleon did not notice him.

Uxbridge's rearguard action
'Well, well', commented Wellington. 'I don't care about the cross-roads now, our infantry are gone.' He then tasked Uxbridge with

fighting a rearguard action to slow the French advance as much as he could and rode off to rejoin the bulk of his army. Uxbridge had with him both heavy and light cavalry, plus horse artillery.

Napoleon was now in a hurry, and put all his energies into driving Uxbridge north as fast as possible. He was worried that Wellington would fall back beyond the Forest of Soignes, which lay south of Brussels, then link up with Blücher to defend Brussels. Barely bothering to deploy for battle, as a cautious commander would, Napoleon advanced on Uxbridge's position.

The task of a rearguard commander was to slow the pursuit of the enemy, and was usually done by deploying as if to contest a river crossing, defile through a wood or steep ridge, forcing the pursuer to stop the chase and himself deploy for action. As soon as a few shots had been exchanged, the rearguard would retreat again and the pursuit would go on. With Napoleon leading forward his cavalry and horse artillery without himself deploying, Uxbridge was hard pushed to slow the chase. Instead, the French were advancing almost as fast as if Uxbridge were not there.

All day long, clouds had been gathering overhead. A little before 3 pm a tremendous clap of thunder reverberated around the landscape. Moments later torrential rain began to fall, drenching uniforms and equipment and making it difficult to fire weapons that used loose gunpowder.

At the small town of Genappe, Uxbridge decided it was time for some real fighting. He appeared to have fallen back out of the town, and the lead units of French light cavalry trotted in. Springing from hiding, Uxbridge threw the 7th Light Dragoons at the French. After a brief tussle, the 7th turned and fled. The jubilant French gave chase, but it was a trap. The British heavy cavalry were waiting just outside the town. As the disordered French light cavalry emerged from the buildings, the heavy cavalry charged home to inflict heavy casualties and drive the French before them. Satisfied that Napoleon would be more cautious next time, Uxbridge continued his retreat.

JEAN-DE-DIEU SOULT

Born in 1769 the son of a rural lawyer, Soult trained as a lawyer but instead joined the army. He gained rapid promotion both under king and republic to become a brigadier general by 1794. He won a string of minor victories in Germany and in 1802 he was given command of Napoleon's bodyguard. He did not like Napoleon, but nevertheless was given high command as a marshal of France. He commanded corps in several major campaigns, including Ulm and Austerlitz, before being sent to Spain, where he fought against Wellington at Talavera in 1809. Although Soult was repulsed in his attacks on the day of battle, Wellington was forced to retreat all the way back to Portugal. Soult then marched on to crush a Spanish army of nearly 60,000 men with his force less than half that size at the Battle of Ocana. This victory opened Spain up to occupation and seemed to ensure French control of that kingdom. Over the next three years, Soult succeeded in stopping the Spanish armies from linking up with Wellington and was managing to hold his own when he fell out with Napoleon's brother Joseph – who had been created king of Spain – and was sacked. Before he left Spain, Soult went through the provinces under his control and stole a vast amount of art treasures. After serving as Napoleon's Chief of Staff in the Waterloo campaign, he fled into exile, but was allowed to return to France in 1819. King Louis XVIII recognized his military talents and made him again a marshal of France. He went on to be minister of war in 1830 and prime minister in 1832–34. In 1838, he attended the coronation of Queen Victoria in London and at the festivities was suddenly grabbed from behind by a man who whispered menacingly 'I've got you at last.' It was a smiling Duke of Wellington. Soult retired in 1848 and died in 1851.

At 6 pm, Wellington received a reply from Blücher to his request for help the following day that had been sent off a little before 10 am. Blücher replied that he would do his best to come the following afternoon with his entire army, but again was not in a position to give a firm time for when he would arrive.

It was a near thing, but night fell just as Napoleon's lead units caught up with the rearmost infantry regiment of Wellington's army – a unit of Brunswickers. Napoleon had reached an inn called *La Belle Alliance* when he saw a ridge around 1.5 km or so ahead of him lined with Wellington's infantry and cavalry. What he could see was only a portion of Wellington's army. Napoleon was uncertain if this was merely a stronger rearguard positioned for the night, or if Wellington was standing to fight and had, as usual, hidden most of his men out of sight. Napoleon sent forward a brigade of cuirassiers, supported by 24 cannon, to find out. They had barely moved forward when a battery of 60 guns boomed out from Wellington's army. Napoleon had his answer. There would be a battle the next day.

As the French army bedded down as well as it could on the damp ground, with thundery showers continuing to sweep overhead, Napoleon received a message from the scouts he had sent out to his right, eastern flank. They had seen in the distance a large body of Prussians marching north towards Wavre from Gembloux. The Prussians had appeared to be in good order, but the French scouts could not be certain due to the distance.

Grouchy's pursuit of Blücher

Napoleon was not overly concerned. He had told Grouchy to hustle Blücher so that he could not regroup, and to stay in touch. To date he had received no message from Grouchy after one written about 3 pm when he said that he was following the Prussians to Gembloux. If anything had gone wrong, Napoleon thought Grouchy would have told him.

In fact, nothing had gone wrong – but nor had very much

gone right. Grouchy had begun by marching toward Gembloux as he was certain that at least a large part of the Prussian army had gone there. The rains began as he marched and before long he found that his artillery and supply wagons were getting stuck in mud with annoying regularity. The road Grouchy was using was of a much poorer quality than the modern, recently paved main road along which Napoleon was following Wellington.

Arriving in Gembloux, Grouchy halted his main body to give the stuck vehicles time to catch up, and meanwhile sent his light cavalry to find out which way the Prussians had gone. It took a long time to establish that although scattered bands of fugitives and baggage had gone east towards Liège and Germany, most of the formed units of fighting men had gone north. The delay was partly caused by the fact that many Prussians were going north without having passed through Gembloux, but having used country roads to the west – which were not probed by Grouchy's cavalry.

If Gneisenau had had his way, the French scouts would have found the Prussian army at Tilly. As it was, most of the Prussians had moved on north toward Wavre, often by roads that did not go through Tilly, and so Grouchy's men missed them. Taking into account the state of the roads, the fact that the Prussians did not appear to be hurrying and the tiredness of his own men, Grouchy decided to stay the night at Gembloux. He reckoned that after a good meal and decent rest, his men would be able to catch up with the Prussians the next day.

Blithely unaware of Grouchy's slow movements, Napoleon was moving among his troops to cheer them up. He was also taking the opportunity to study Wellington's position – and he was puzzled. The ridge on which Wellington had positioned his army was not particularly steep, nor very high. A short distance behind it was the huge Forest of Soignes. Moving an army through a wood could be tricky, especially if the troops were being harried by an enemy. The ridge therefore appeared to be both difficult to hold and difficult to retreat from. Twice that night Napoleon got out of bed to go and look at Wellington's position for signs of a retreat. At 3.30 am, some men he had sent forward disguised as local peasants returned to report that Wellington's army was asleep. There would be no retreat.

Napoleon was relieved. He had 75,000 men to Wellington's 67,000. His men were all experienced veterans, many of Wellington's were raw recruits. Blücher was miles away and battered, while Grouchy was – Napoleon thought – blocking his path to Wellington. The next day would be bloody, no doubt, but also victorious.

Henry Paget, Earl of Uxbridge

Henry Paget was born into one of the richest and noblest families in Britain, his father being both Earl of Uxbridge and Baron Paget, a title that went back to 1553. With his family's wealth and connections, Henry could have chosen any profession. After trying politics as MP for Caernarvon, he opted for the military. He began in the infantry in 1793, but transferred to the cavalry in 1797 and began a career of rapid promotion. The Battle of Castricum of 1799 saw him fighting alongside Russian allies in the Netherlands against the French. The battle ended in defeat, though Paget was considered to have handled his men well. In 1808, he was promoted to lieutenant-general and went to the Spanish peninsula to command the British cavalry. He showed enormous skill in advance guard and rearguard actions, and gained fame with his cavalry raid on Sahagún. His handling of the rearguard cavalry has been credited with saving the main British army during its retreat to Corunna, from whence it was evacuated by the Royal Navy.

He was earmarked to return to Portugal under Wellington, but while at home in England he abandoned his wife and ran off with Lady Charlotte Wellesley, wife of Wellington's brother, Henry. This understandably soured relations between him and Wellington and he was removed from the Peninsula by the government. In 1810, he and Lady Charlotte divorced their respective spouses and married. When Napoleon landed in France, Uxbridge was considered the best choice to command the British cavalry, but he was appointed only after Wellington had been consulted. The two men had not rekindled their former friendship, but were able to work together well during the campaign.

CHAPTER 7

'AN OPENING IN THE LINE THUS OCCURRED'

Captain Duthilt of the French 45th Infantry, writing some years after the battle

The position taken up by Wellington just south of Waterloo appeared at first glance to be a simple ridge, but there were distinct features that would come to be crucial in the battle as it unfolded.

The Mont-Saint-Jean ridge ran at right angles to the main road heading north to Brussels, along which Wellington had retreated the previous day. That main road ran direct from La Belle Alliance, the inn where Napoleon had his battlefield base, to the top of the Mont-Saint-Jean ridge, where Wellington had his. The two headquarters were separated by around 1,200 m. In that space the land fell gently down into a valley before climbing up again to Mont-Saint-Jean.

The land was open and unbroken by hedges, ditches or trees. Most of the ground was covered by standing crops of grain, which stood 1.5–2 m tall. In the earlier stages of the battle these would hinder the view of the men on the ground, but before long it would be trampled flat. The fields were generally flat, but in places there were small rises and dips. At the eastern end of the battlefield the small Smohain stream cut through a narrow valley that was deeper than the rest of the battlefield. The stream ran north-east to join the river Dyle near Wavre.

Along the top of Wellington's ridge ran a poor-quality country road from Wavre to Hal. Where it crossed the main road to Brussels there stood a large elm tree – where Wellington took up his position. To the east of the crossroads, this road was lined by hedges; to the west, it ran through a cutting. Both features offered some protection to infantry, so Wellington put his first line along this road.

Defensive positions

Three substantial farm complexes stood in the valley between the two ridges. These buildings were all of stone and could be made into impressive defensive positions. Men stationed in the farms would be able to pour flanking fire into any French columns seeking to bypass them to attack Wellington on his ridge. They were therefore crucial to Wellington's defensive plans.

In the east, on Wellington's left flank, was Papelotte. This stood at the head of the ravine carrying the Smohain stream. Wellington stationed men of Perponcher's Dutch division in Papelotte to defend it. Further out to the left was the hamlet of Frischermont, but this played little role in the battle.

Standing immediately beside the main Brussels road was La Haye Sainte. This consisted of a substantial house together with stables and a barn all linked by a high stone wall that enclosed a courtyard with a pond. A gate gave access from the courtyard to the main road, but otherwise only a few windows looked out from the complex. Wellington put two battalions of the King's German Legion into La Haye Sainte, supported by a Nassau regiment behind them.

On the opposite side of the main road, facing La Haye Sainte, was a hillock that had been largely excavated by locals carting off the fine sand of which it was composed. Into this sandpit were put the 95th Rifles. This regiment was equipped with the Baker rifle, which was far more accurate than the standard infantry musket, but which was slow to load and often suffered from jamming. The most westerly of the farms was also the largest. Hougoumont is usually described as a 'chateau', meaning it was a country manor rather than a farmhouse. Like La Haye Sainte, it was built around a walled courtyard, but the buildings were bigger and more solid. In addition to the main house, there was a chapel, barn, stable, cottages and assorted outbuildings. A gate opened to the south and another to the north. To the east of the buildings was a walled, formal garden with an orchard, also walled, to the east of the garden. To the south of the complex was a wood surrounded by substantial hedges. To garrison this stronghold, Wellington put the light companies of the four regiments of British Guards who were present.

Wellington remained concerned about his right wing, worrying that Napoleon might yet march west to cut him off from his supply lines and the Royal Navy. He put most of his army to the west of the main road, massing in the right half of his line. Even that was not enough. A detached force of around 15,000 men was put at Hal, several kilometres to the west, where it guarded the road back to the Scheldt. It was there to guard his route to safety should Blücher not come to Waterloo in time. At 2 am Wellington received a letter from Blücher in which the Prussian stated that his men were so tired that they could not start to march until dawn. As the sun came up, however, Blücher would put Bülow's IV Corps in motion, followed by the other corps as soon as they could be got formed up and moving. Looking at a map, Wellington judged that Bülow might arrive about 2 pm.

Morning plans – fraught exchanges
Both Wellington and Napoleon were up and on the field by dawn. Wellington moved a few units about until he was satisfied, then he took up position under the elm tree at the crossroads, from where he had an excellent view of the area, and waited.

There he was approached by a succession of senior commanders seeking advice or passing on news. One such conversation was with Uxbridge, the commander of the British cavalry and second most senior officer on the field. Uxbridge had a delicate question to ask. Wellington was notoriously secretive and had not discussed his plans for the coming battle. 'Since I am second in command: should anything happen to you, what are your plans?' Uxbridge asked.

Wellington indicated the gathering French army ahead of them. 'Who will attack first,' he asked, 'Bonaparte or us?'

'Bonaparte,' replied Uxbridge.

'Well,' continued Wellington, 'Bonaparte has not given me a copy of his plans and since my plans depend on what he does, how can you expect me to tell you what my plans are?' Uxbridge withdrew, chastened.

Napoleon was keen to get the battle started. At 6 am he dictated to Soult general movement orders for his troops, stating that the regiments should move at 9 am. While his army moved into position, Napoleon had breakfast with his senior officers. Men came and went as their duties allowed, but in any case it turned out to be a fraught meal. Napoleon had been expounding on how the odds were in his favour when Ney entered and caught the end of his remarks. Ney said that when he had fought Wellington in Spain the British general had proved adept at slipping out of apparently secure traps. Soult, who had also faced Wellington before, chipped in to suggest that a message be sent to Grouchy asking him to detach Gérard's corps to march across country to fall on Wellington's left flank.

Napoleon threw down his cutlery in anger. 'Because you have been beaten by Wellington, you consider him a great general. I tell you that he is a bad general, that the English are bad troops and this affair is nothing more serious than eating breakfast.' A tense silence followed, broken when Reille and Napoleon's brother Jérôme entered. Napoleon turned to Reille – who had also fought the British in Spain – and asked him for his opinion of the British army. The hapless Reille, unaware of the previous exchange, replied: 'Well posted, as Wellington knows how to post it, and attacked from the front, I consider the English infantry to be impregnable because of their tenacity and superior firing. Doing that, we can expect to suffer heavy casualties. But the English are less agile, less supple and less skilled in manoeuvring than we are. We cannot defeat them by direct attack, but we can beat them by manoeuvring.'

Napoleon glowered. Sensing something was amiss, Jérôme tried to lighten the mood by passing on some gossip. The waiter who had served him supper the night before at an inn had made the ridiculous statement that an English officer had said that Blücher would arrive by noon next day.

Again Napoleon burst out angrily. 'I am delighted the English are going to fight. This battle will save France. I will use my preponderance of artillery to batter Wellington, then I will probe with my cavalry to unmask his position, then I will march straight through him with my Guard.' With that he stormed off, beckoning Soult to join him and began issuing a string of orders.

His first order was to Grouchy. Unaware that the main Prussian army had retreated to Wavre and thinking that only a relatively small group was in that town, Napoleon instructed Grouchy to 'head for Wavre so that you get close to us and establish close communications with us while pushing ahead of you those portions of the Prussian army that have gone to Wavre. Do this as soon as possible.'

Napoleon's second order was to the commanding officer of the 7th Hussars. He was instructed to lead his regiment out to the east and post a screen of scouts over a wide area so as to keep an eye open for any troops – French or Prussian – approaching from Wavre. Finally he turned to issuing detailed orders for the assault on Wellington.

Meanwhile, perturbed by Napoleon's casual attitude to launching a frontal assault on British infantry, several of the senior French generals went into a huddle to compare notes on fighting the British and seek a way forward. They all had experience of leading infantry in columns against British infantry drawn up in lines. Against other continental armies the massed momentum of large columns had been enough to smash a path to victory. But the better-trained British infantry had stood firm and defeated them with volleys of musketry.

D'Erlon, Reille, Lobau and Drouet decided to adopt an unusual formation known as *colonne de division par bataillon*, which was used only very occasionally by the French. This was a mixed formation in which some men were arranged in column, while others were in smaller groups that could be deployed into line quickly to add their firepower to the momentum of the columns. The number of muskets that could be fired by a division in this formation was about 350, compared to just 60 in a conventional column. The downside was that the formation was rather cumbersome and difficult to manoeuvre over broken ground.

The mud meanwhile had forced Napoleon to delay his assault. The heavy cannon could not be moved over the muddy fields. The attack was postponed to 11 am, then to 12 noon.

Attack on Hougoumont
To fill in the time, and in the hope of inducing Wellington to weaken his centre, Napoleon told Reille to start a small attack on Hougoumont. Napoleon guessed that Wellington would be anxious about his right wing and the escape route to the Royal Navy. He therefore intended to tease him there. Should Hougoumont be captured it would open the way for a sweeping flank march by Napoleon to get between Wellington and his escape. Napoleon did not intend to make such a move, but by threatening to do so he hoped to get Wellington to move more men to the apparently threatened flank.

The French attack on Hougoumont was led by Napoleon's brother, Jérôme. Barely had the assault begun than Jérôme's right-hand man, General Bauduin, was shot dead. It took an hour for the French skirmishers to drive the Hanoverian light infantry out of the large wood in front of the chateau itself. The first assault on the buildings was made against the high, loopholed south wall and was beaten off with heavy losses. Jérôme then fell back into the wood, while bringing up more men

HONORÉ REILLE

Born in 1775, Reille served in several campaigns in the Revolutionary Wars, but made his mark when appointed Governor of Florence in 1800. At the time, the various small states of Italy were being reorganized to ease the spread of the ideals of the French Revolution. After a year, Florence was incorporated into the new Kingdom of Etruria, a client state of France. After some months as an aide de camp to Napoleon himself, Reille was sent to Germany on a delicate mission.

As part of his redrawing of the map of Europe, Napoleon had abolished the Holy Roman Empire and abolished many of the small states within it. In 1806, the Duchy of Wurttemburg was rewarded for its support of French ambitions by being elevated to the status of a kingdom and given control over numerous formerly free cities and ecclesiastical territories. However, Napoleon did not entirely trust the new King Frederick, so Reille was given command of the Württemberg army and a position at court. Then, in 1808, Napoleon sent him to Spain to act as governor of Aragon where his administrative skills were intended to bring peace and stability. There, Reille enjoyed some success in pacifying his area, but in 1813 was defeated by Wellington at Vitoria. He thereafter played a secondary role in the remaining battles of the Peninsular War.

After the fall of Napoleon, Reille served Louis XVIII before defecting to Napoleon at the first opportunity. After Waterloo he briefly went into exile, but returned in 1819 to become a peer of France. He held a series of military positions until promoted to be Marshal of France in 1852. He died in 1860 in Paris at the age of 84 and was given a formal funeral.

and ordering them around the west side of the chateau to attack the north wall.

Wellington did not want to change his dispositions until it was clear whether the attack on Hougoumont was a real attack or a feint. He did, however, push forward a battery of howitzers to fire explosive shells over the chateau into the woods beyond. Otherwise he did not fall into the trap that Napoleon had laid.

French cannon

The main battle opened when a massed battery of 84 cannon fired as one a little before noon. The massive noise of so many guns firing at once stunned those on the battlefield and was heard by both Grouchy and Blücher.

Grouchy was, at this point, marching north toward Wavre. His progress was slow, partly because of the poor state of the road but also because he had delayed his departure from Gembloux until he was certain that Blücher had gone to Wavre. He had sent a letter to Napoleon on leaving Gembloux, and this arrived with Napoleon as the attack on Hougoumont got underway. Napoleon was aghast to learn that Grouchy was moving so slowly. He sent an immediate reply telling Grouchy to get a move on, specifically telling him to get between Wavre and Waterloo. Napoleon knew this message would not reach Grouchy for a couple of hours, but speed was now of the essence.

Meanwhile, French scouts had captured a Prussian hussar carrying a message from Blücher to Wellington. It was a routine update on Bülow's progress, but it was the first time Napoleon realized that the Prussians were marching on Waterloo. Napoleon hurriedly discussed the news with Soult, whereupon the grinning Prussian chipped in, speaking reasonable French, to boast that the entire Prussian army was on the march.

Napoleon moved Lobau's VI Corps forward to his right flank to face east on a line from Frischermont in the north to

Plancenoit in the south. They would halt the Prussians, or at least delay them long enough to allow Napoleon to defeat Wellington.

The vast battery of 84 cannon had, meanwhile, been pounding Wellington's centre on both sides of the crossroads. They were firing both solid shot and shells to increase the damage done. As usual, Wellington had put his men behind the crest of the hill both to shelter them from cannon fire and to hide his dispositions from the enemy. Nevertheless, Napoleon had guessed where Wellington would have his main force and was directing his fire at it. Although many shot and shells hit the front of the ridge and sank into the mud, many of them went over the ridge to strike the men beyond.

Casualties among Wellington's army were not so high as they would have been if he had put his men on the forward slope in the continental manner, but they were still high. Infantry regiments were ordered to sit or lie down to try to reduce casualties, while the cavalry were moved back or to the side.

French infantry attack

At 1.30 pm, Napoleon judged that Wellington's army must have suffered enough casualties to have weakened their line and reduced morale. D'Erlon's I Corps marched forward to attack. More than 15,000 infantry were marching forward, their front protected by a swarm of skirmishers and their flanks by heavy cavalry.

One French brigade was earmarked to attack the farm of La Haye Sainte. After a delay caused by the fire of the British 95th Rifles in the sandpit, the French fell on the farm and its King's German Legion defenders. Led by Major Baring, the Germans

Opposite: The initial assault on Hougoumont. A few British infantry were stationed outside the chateau proper, defending the orchard and walled garden. Once the size of the French attack became clear they fell back into the buildings.

had found the farm in a terrible condition for defence. The main gate had been chopped up for firewood, so only the flimsiest of barricades blocked the main entrance. Baring had 400 men, the French had 2,000.

Before long La Haye Sainte was surrounded by French infantry, who captured the orchard and were battering at the gates. On the ridge behind the farm, the Prince of Orange saw the farm surrounded. Realizing that the main attack of d'Erlon would pass to his east, the prince decided to send a Hanoverian infantry regiment to the rescue. Intent on the French infantry, the prince sent the regiment forward in line formation. Suddenly erupting from the smoke of the fighting around La Haye Sainte came a regiment of French cuirassiers, which charged into the Hanoverians and slaughtered them.

The main French column, meanwhile, had been slogging up the slope towards Wellington's line. It was formed into three sections. On the left was Quiot's division, in the centre was Donzelot's and on the right was Marcognet's division. For the final few minutes, the French battery redoubled its efforts to deluge the defenders with explosive shells to inflict as many casualties as they could and damage morale as much as possible.

As Donzelot's French infantry crested the ridge they found themselves facing Dutch troops commanded by Major General van Bijlandt. Using their novel formation, the French could fire more muskets than usual. A crashing volley inflicted heavy casualties on the Dutch, who had already taken losses at Quatre Bras. When the French came on with fixed bayonets it proved to be too much. Bijlandt's men fled. There was a gap in the line.

Opposite: General Thomas Picton was a blunt, plain-speaking officer who rarely wasted time on small talk or on subtle battlefield manoeuvres. Although shown here in formal uniform, he preferred to wear a civilian outfit on campaign and was in a black frock coat when he was killed at Waterloo.

Seeing this, General Picton began leading forward some British infantry, but was shot dead by a bullet that went through his hat and smashed into his skull.

Quiot's left-hand French column met the British infantry under Sir James Kempt and a fierce firefight developed. The British had the advantage of lining the hedges along the road that ran east–west along the crest of the ridge. Even so, with the French in their new formations both sides could deploy about 2,000 muskets and were evenly matched.

To Bijlandt's left, the British redcoats were also being struck by d'Erlon's novel formation. The 92nd Highlanders took heavy casualties and fell back. As they gave way, the 92nd disrupted the formation of the 44th behind them and both units gave ground. With fixed bayonets, Marcognet's infantry surged forward into the gap. To their left was Donzelot's division, also marching forward through the gap they had created.

Some of Marcognet's men began to shout 'Victoire' as they saw the open ground ahead of them. The officers began to redeploy their infantry so that they could turn to take those British regiments still fighting in the flank – and defeat them. Now was the time for the French heavy cavalry. Their task was to surge through the gap created by d'Erlon's skilful infantry attack to fan out and smash Wellington's troops from the rear. However, from where they were – to the right rear of the French infantry – the cuirassiers could not see what was happening due to the smoke and the lie of the land. Napoleon could see, and sent a galloper forward to tell Brigadier François Wathiez to charge forward and destroy Wellington.

Also able to see what was happening, but a good deal closer to the action, was the Earl of Uxbridge. He hurriedly ordered Lord Edward Somerset, who commanded the elite heavy cavalry Household Brigade, to prepare to charge, then spurred over to Sir William Ponsonby of the Union Brigade to give him the same order, backed by the instruction to follow Somerset as soon as his men moved off. Galloping back to Somerset, Uxbridge hurriedly surveyed the scene. He knew that if he got into the gap before the French heavy cavalry he would be able to catch the French infantry as they were redeploying. If not, then the battle would be lost. Waving his sabre, he gave the order to charge.

CHAPTER 8

'GALLOPING AT EVERYTHING'

Wellington speaking about British cavalry after the Battle of Maguilla in 1812. The full quote is: 'Our officers of cavalry have acquired the trick of galloping at everything. They never consider the situation, never think of manoeuvring before an enemy, and never keep back or provide for a reserve.'

First of the British heavy cavalry to move were the Life Guards, led by Uxbridge himself, with the 1st Dragoon Guards to their left and the Horse Guards behind in support. Spurring to a trot, then a canter and gallop, this force of more than 1,000 large men on large horses poured through the spaces in the line held by the Prince of Orange to the west of the main road to Brussels.

Leaping over the hedges to their front, the tide of rushing horsemen crashed into the small group of cuirassiers who had just scattered the Hanoverians sent forward by the Prince of Orange. Disorganized by their own success, the French were thrown aside. Some fell over the steep bank where the Brussels Road cut through the rise of the ridge and tumbled down – men and horses lost their lives. The fight between the two sets of elite heavy cavalrymen provided a highpoint in the cavalry action.

The Horse Guards and Dragoon Guards continued on down the slope west of La Haye Sainte. Brushing aside other French cavalry they reached the infantry still trying to smash a way into the courtyard. They, too, were thrown back by the triumphant heavy horsemen. Somerset slowly got his men under control. Having secured the approaches to La Haye Sainte and made sure that Baring and his men were safe, Somerset led his regiments back up the slope.

They had not got halfway up the slope, when Somerset saw more French horsemen. Charging again, Somerset drove into two brigades of cuirassiers and took them utterly by surprise. The French scattered and fled. Again Somerset got his men in hand and returned to where he had started.

Uxbridge, meanwhile, had wheeled the Life Guards to their left. He led them in a spirited charge across the face of the ridge north of La Haye Sainte to crash into the flank of the French infantry of Quiot. The sudden charge slammed into the French men exchanging fire with the British infantry along the hedges. An officer of the British infantry who had been taking heavy casualties later recorded the sudden and unexpected impact of Uxbridge and his men:

'The infantry to our front gave way, followed by the Life Guards who were cutting away in all directions. Hundreds of the infantry threw themselves down and pretended to be dead while the cavalry galloped over them, and then they got up and ran away.'

Uxbridge re-formed his men in time to see another French brigade of infantry coming up the hill out of the smoke. Wheeling almost as calmly as if on parade, Uxbridge charged again, causing the French infantry to turn and run back down the slope. There was then some confusion as the British infantry came running down the slope with bayonets fixed. In the smoke and disorder the British officers mistook the blue French uniforms for blue Dutch uniforms. The chase was called off, allowing far more Frenchmen to escape than would otherwise have been the case.

While all this was taking place, Ponsonby had seen the Household Brigade start forward and had ordered his trumpeter to sound the charge. On his right were the Royal Dragoon Guards, in his centre came the Inniskilling Dragoons and on his left the Scots Greys. It was the English, Irish and Scottish nationalities of the regiments that gave the unit its name – the Union Brigade.

The Scots Greys on the left had been sheltering from the cannon fire in a dip in the ground. As they spurred up the slope out of the dip to reach the crest of the ridge they ran headlong into the lead units of Marcognet's division. To the Frenchmen it seemed as if the huge men on grey horses had erupted straight out of the earth. There was no time for the French to get into square, nor even to see what was happening before the Greys were upon them.

One French officer recorded how he had been intent on organizing his men to fire at the disintegrating British infantry when:

'I turned to push one of my men into position when I was amazed to see him fall dead at my feet from a sabre slash. I turned round instantly to see British cavalry forcing their way into our formation and hacking us to pieces.'

So dense was the French column that the Scots Greys were slowed to a walk as they butchered their way through. Seeing the change of fortunes, the scattered men of 92nd turned and – entirely without orders – charged at the French with their bayonets fixed. The carnage was frightful.

Eagle of the Empire

As the slaughter proceeded, Sergeant Charles Ewart had just killed a French officer when he realized that he was next to a French flag. At this date the capture of a flag was an achievement of great honour, and the loss of one a great disgrace. This particular flag was no ordinary banner, but an Eagle of the Empire. When he became emperor in 1805, Napoleon had

Opposite: The final act in the dramatic assault on Wellington's centre by the vast French infantry columns led by d'Erlon. The Scots Greys, having smashed through the infantry, went too far down the hill and found themselves exposed to a flank attack by French lancers while their path was blocked by cuirassiers.

presented each regiment in the French army with a gilded bronze eagle mounted on a pole, to which was attached a French flag. Many of these had been destroyed by Louis XVIII, but Napoleon made a point of having new ones made and issued to the regiments in time for the campaign of 1815.

Ewart grabbed the flag and yanked it, causing the man who held it to turn on him. Using his height on his horse and enormous physical strength, Ewart unbalanced the Frenchman, then hacked him down with his sabre. Another Frenchman at once attacked Ewart, but he, too, was killed. A wounded Frenchman on the ground then shot his musket at Ewart, but missed. Ewart then rode back to the ridge to report his achievement to an officer.

The Inniskillings and Royals slammed head on into Donzelot's men who had scattered the Dutch. One squadron of the Royals were unable to get through the hedges, and had to stop, move to the left and reform before continuing their charge. They were therefore some distance behind their comrades.

The rest of the Royals and Inniskillings crashed into the French infantry, bursting open their formation and doing as much damage as the Greys had done. Captain Kennedy of the Royals reported what happened next:

'I did not see the eagle and colour (for there were two colours, but only one with an eagle) until we had been probably five or six minutes engaged. It must, I should think, have been originally about the centre of the column, and got uncovered from the change of direction. When I first saw it, it was perhaps about forty yards to my left and a little in my front. The officer who carried it and his companions were moving in the direction, with their backs towards me, and endeavouring to force their way into the crowd. I gave the order to my squadron, "Right shoulders forward, attack the colour", leading direct on the point myself. On reaching it, I ran my sword into the officer's right side a little above his hip joint. He was a little to my left side, and he fell to that side with the eagle across my horse's head. I tried to catch it with my left hand, but could only touch the fringe of the

flag, and it is probable it would have fallen to the ground, had it not been prevented by the neck of Corporal Styles' horse, who came up close to my left at the instant, and against which it fell. Corporal Styles was Standard Coverer; his post was immediately behind me, and his duty to follow wherever I led. When I first saw the eagle I gave the order "Right shoulders forward, attack the colour", and on running the officer through the body I called out twice together "Secure the colour, secure the colour, it belongs to me." This order was addressed to some men close to me, of whom Corporal Styles was one. On taking up the eagle, I endeavoured to break the eagle from the pole with the intention of putting it into the breast of my coat; but I could not break it. Corporal Styles said "Pray, sir, do not break it," on which I replied "Very well, carry it to the rear as fast as you can, it belongs to me."'

Having hacked their way through Marcognet's men the Scots Greys careered on down the slope. Seeing them come, a reserve French brigade commanded by Comte Pierre Durutte formed square. The Greys made little impression, but rode past as the French fired and emptied several saddles.

Moments later the squadron of the Royals that had been delayed came rampaging down the hill and struck Durutte's square before his men had time to reload their muskets. They cut their way into the square, the men of which promptly turned and fled with the vengeful horsemen killing anyone they could reach.

Ponsonby was now trying to rally his men. His regiments had come farther down the slope than those of Somerset and were considerably more disordered from having fought their way through dense infantry formations. It was then that the heavy cavalry sent forward by Napoleon to exploit d'Erlon's success arrived on the scene. Cheated of their expected victory, the cuirassiers fell vengefully on the exhausted British cavalry. Another French cavalry unit, the lancers of the Imperial Guard, had been stationed on the far right near Papelotte and the ravine of the Smohain stream. Their commander saw the cuirassiers attacking the tired British cavalry and led his lancers to join in.

Ponsonby was cut down by a lancer when his heavy horse got stuck in a muddy ploughed field, and hundreds of his men were similarly killed by the lancers and cuirassiers. Baron Gighny, leader of the Dutch light cavalry, spurred forward with his two regiments to join the fray, followed by Sir John Vandeleur with three regiments of British light cavalry.

The arrival of the British and Dutch light cavalry decided the issue and the French withdrew. The opening phase of the battle was over by about 3 pm. D'Erlon's massive and innovative attack had come very close to success. The French had opened up a clear hole in the centre of Wellington's army, but the charge of the British heavy cavalry had thrown them back.

Bruising encounter

The casualties on both sides had been heavy. Of d'Erlon's infantry about 2,000 were dead and 3,000 taken prisoner, with hundreds more wounded. Some units had taken particularly heavy casualties, and even those that had escaped relatively lightly were disorganized and scattered. It would take some time before d'Erlon had any infantry regiments able to fight with any real cohesion.

The British cavalry had started their charge with some 2,500 men and horses. More than half of these had been killed or wounded. The Scots Greys suffered especially badly. They had started with 416 men and horses: now 228 horses were dead along with 104 men, while another 97 were so badly wounded that they had to leave the field for hospital treatment. Among the British cavalry regiments there now followed a reorganization, as wounded men gave up their horses to unwounded, but horseless comrades. Like d'Erlon's infantry it would be some time before they were fit to fight again.

Napoleon was aware that time was running out. He did not know exactly where Bülow was, but he knew the Prussian was on his way. He had little time to defeat Wellington, but if

Wellington could be defeated then Napoleon could turn to face Bülow with all his force. With Grouchy hopefully cutting across country toward Waterloo it was likely that Bülow would be caught between the two French forces and crushed.

The entire campaign depended on Napoleon being able to defeat Wellington before Bülow arrived.

CHAPTER 9

'GIVE ME NIGHT OR GIVE ME BLÜCHER'

Wellington, on the field of Waterloo

While d'Erlon's attack was unfolding, Reille's corps had become increasingly drawn into the fighting around Hougoumont. This had been prompted by Prince Jérôme's decision to lead a second brigade of infantry into the assault on the chateau.

The high point of this assault came when French infantry, working round the western side of the buildings, managed to reach the north gate at a time when it had been opened to allow ammunition to be brought in from the ridge. There was a rush on both sides, the British trying to close the gate, the French trying to get through before it closed.

Heroism at Hougoumont

The British got the gate closed in time, but Sous-Lieutenant Legros had an axe and used it to smash his way inside. This huge officer charged in, followed by about 50 of his comrades. Lieutenant Colonel James Macdonnell of the Coldstream Guards together with Corporal James Graham and a handful of others ran back to the gates and managed to shut them again by pushing with brute force against the press of Frenchmen outside. All the Frenchmen inside the farm were killed, except for the drummer boy, who was trussed up and thrown into the farm chapel. In the fighting Corporal Graham saved the life of his captain by killing a Frenchman who was about to shoot the officer.

Wellington later remarked that the battle had hinged on closing the gates at Hougoumont. Corporal Graham was promoted to sergeant by his colonel for his bravery, and subsequently on the recommendation of Wellington was given an annuity that he received until his death in 1845.

Soon after the closing of the gates, Macdonnell realized that his men were low on ammunition. He gave the agreed signal that he needed to be resupplied and a driver of the wagon train set off down the hill with a cartload of ammunition. To reach Hougoumont he had to cross several hundred yards of open ground, swept by French artillery fire and within musket range of the French infantry. He got through, but every horse was injured and the cart was a wreck.

This sort of growing battle was not what Napoleon had intended. He fully appreciated the tactical importance of the chateau and that capturing it would allow him to outflank Wellington's right wing. However, he had not intended to launch such an attack, but to batter his way through Wellington's centre. The intention had been to worry Wellington and trick him into moving troops away from the centre to protect his right. Wellington had not done so, but nor had he moved any of the men on his right to reinforce his centre.

Napoleon ordered that a battery of howitzers should be brought up to fire incendiary shells into the farm with the purpose of setting fire to the buildings. He was hoping to achieve his purpose without the need to feed more men into the growing struggle. The shells soon had the buildings on fire – indeed, only the chapel would not eventually go up in flames.

As the flames got a hold, Wellington sent Macdonnell a message: 'I see that the fire has communicated itself from the haystack to the roof. You must, however, keep your men in those parts to which the fire does not reach. Take care that no men are lost by the falling in of the roof or floors. After they have fallen in, occupy the ruined walls inside the Garden, particularly if it should be possible for the enemy to pass through the embers in the inside of the House.' Wellington was determined to hold Hougoumont.

Artillery onslaught

With his plan for the battle in disarray, Napoleon now had to think quickly to achieve a breakthrough. He ordered his grand battery of over 80 guns to open fire again, swamping the central area of Wellington's ridge with cannonballs and explosive shells. One British officer was wounded by a ball and fell to the ground. Six of his men rushed forward with a blanket to carry him to the rear for medical treatment when a shell came down and killed them all. In the ranks of the 40th Regiment an exploding shell hurled a man 2 m into the air, over the heads of his alarmed colleagues to land in a tangled heap behind them. Amazingly, he was unwounded. Elsewhere, men were falling in numbers; again regiments were told to lie down to avoid casualties and the cavalry were pulled back.

On the French side of the valley, Napoleon was engaged in a not dissimilar operation. Many of d'Erlon's units had taken relatively few casualties, but had become scattered and disorganized. Men needed to be recalled to their colours and got into formation. Those units that had taken heavy casualties also needed sorting out and the fitter men reformed in new formations.

A message arrived from Grouchy. It had been written at 11 am from the village of Walhain. The first thing this told Napoleon was that Grouchy was moving forward to Wavre, not cutting across country toward Waterloo; it also showed that Grouchy was moving slowly. The contents of the letter claimed that Blücher had halted near Wavre, but that Grouchy thought they were about to retreat back to Brussels to which place Grouchy would chase them. Clearly at 11 am Grouchy had not yet got Napoleon's new orders. Whether he yet had them and what he was doing about them Napoleon had no way of knowing. He could only hope that Grouchy was doing what he had been told and was cutting across country.

Napoleon decided that before a fresh attack on Wellington could be launched the farm of La Haye Sainte had to be captured.

Ney sent in a brigade of infantry, which as it advanced suffered badly from the sniping of the 95th Rifles who had reoccupied the sandpit. Again the French took the orchard, but could get no further and failed to capture the farmhouse.

Exactly who took the decision about what to do next is unclear. Some accounts say it was Ney who took the decision as Napoleon was temporarily ill with stomach cramps at the time. Others maintain that Ney could not have taken such a drastic decision without Napoleon's approval. Whoever gave the orders, what followed was one of the most dramatic episodes in Napoleonic warfare.

French cavalry charge

Napoleon had few infantry reserves except for the Imperial Guard, which he had always used only for a decisive, victorious blow. In front of him was Wellington with a greatly diminished and badly battered army. Somewhere to his right – he did not know where – were Blücher and Grouchy, both marching cross-country to join the battle. Napoleon needed to destroy Wellington quickly so that he could turn his forces east to join with Grouchy and destroy Blücher in turn. The militarily sensible option of withdrawing to link up with Grouchy and try again was not open to Napoleon because he needed a quick victory to break apart the coalition ranged against him.

The only large force of men available to him was his cavalry. Using cavalry to assault an army not yet broken by infantry attacks was a risky move. Other commanders had used the move before, generally with unfortunate results, but Napoleon had triumphantly used cavalry in this way at the Battle of Eylau in 1807. In that battle, Napoleon had also found himself without infantry reserves, though this time facing a Russian army; somewhere nearby there had been a Prussian army, with a French force under Ney also in the area.

Napoleon had ordered Murat to assault the Russian centre with a vast force of cavalry: Murat had smashed his way through the

Russian centre, inflicting heavy casualties and throwing the Russian formations into disarray. Although the Russians had brought up reserves to plug the gap, the delay had been sufficient to allow Ney to arrive on the Russian flank. Napoleon had won the battle, and soon after forced Russia to make peace.

At Waterloo, Napoleon knew that Wellington had no reserves left on the field. A similar massed cavalry charge might very well deliver him victory. But Napoleon had two handicaps that he had not faced at Eylau. First, he was attacking the well-trained, professional British infantry, not the conscripted Russians. Second, he did not have Murat with him to lead the charge. Handling large numbers of heavy cavalry in action was a difficult thing to do. Murat could manage it, not least because the French cavalry loved and respected him, but few others could do so. The British heavy cavalry had just achieved great things, but had ended up taking huge casualties because their officers had been unable to rally them.

Now Ney was about to lead one of the greatest cavalry assaults in history.

Whether he would be able to control his men remained to be seen. He brought up the IV Cavalry Corps of 3,000 cuirassiers and the Guard light cavalrymen, as many men again, to a position between La Haye Sainte and Hougoumont.

Wellington watched Ney's horsemen gathering to attack with puzzlement. When fighting the French in Spain, Wellington had rarely faced large numbers of French cavalry, and those he had met had been less than useful due to the often mountainous terrain. He had studied reports of Napoleon's battles, but had little first-hand experience of what French cavalry could do. He ordered his infantry to form squares on the reverse of the ridge.

Opposite: French heavy cavalry charge the squares of British infantry, but after a few exchanges of fire, both sides fell back on cold steel as sabre faced bayonet. The artillery shown here forming part of a square were, in fact, stationed between the squares.

BATTLE OF WATERLOO.

W. Jones, Pinxt.

Published & Sold April 11 1816 by Edw.d Orme, Publisher to His Majesty & H.R.H. the Prince Regent, Bond Street, corner of Brook Street, London.

The artillerymen were to fire into advancing horsemen for as long as possible, then run to take shelter in the squares. Wellington's cavalry were to pull back to well behind the infantry squares and watch for an opportunity to launch a counter-attack.

Ney led his vast cavalry force up the slope at a trot, breaking into a canter as they approached the British guns so as to cover the deadly ground quickly while still keeping formation. When the British guns fired their shot and grapeshot they inflicted casualties on the horsemen, but the vast majority of the French got through. Among those to go down was Ney himself. He was not injured, but his horse was killed. Streaked with mud, Ney grabbed a horse off a passing man and leapt back into the saddle, spurring up the hill to catch up with the lead units.

As the French cavalry surged over the crest of the ridge they saw spread out ahead of them a patchwork of British and Dutch infantry in squares. The squares relied on the bristling hedge of bayonets to keep the horses at bay. Once the men had fired their muskets, therefore, they could not reload without withdrawing their bayonets from the hedge and giving the French an opening. After one volley the squares fell silent.

The horsemen had a pair of heavy pistols each. These fired a ball nearly as large as that of a musket, but had a shorter range. Once the cavalry had fired their pistols, they too were reluctant to take the time to reload so their firearms fell silent. The sabres of the cuirassiers were shorter than the infantry bayonets, so in the clash of cold steel that followed the infantry had the longer reach, while the cavalry moved with greater speed and nimbleness. When the lancers came up, they found that they could outreach the bayonets and inflicted greater casualties.

Pounding of cannon

Having failed to break the squares, Ney and his horsemen fell back down the slope. Napoleon then opened fire again with his grand battery of cannon. This time the damage the artillery did was even greater. Infantry in squares were densely packed so any cannonball hitting them would kill or disable half a dozen men, while an exploding shell might kill a dozen or more.

After allowing the guns to pound Wellington's infantry for some time, Ney returned to the charge. Again his men took casualties from British artillery and muskets, while inflicting death on their own account with their pistols and lances. But once more the squares held firm. A counter-charge by British light cavalry sent Ney back down the hill again, but opened the way for the French artillery to open fire with renewed fury.

During the lull in the cavalry attacks, the commanders of the British 30th and 73rd Regiments combined their men into one square after both lost so many men that their individual squares were too small to be firm. Wellington realized his men were taking heavy punishment and could not hold out for much longer. He was heard to mutter 'Give me night, or give me Blücher'.

At around 5 pm, Napoleon sent Ney reinforcements in the shape of Kellerman's III Cavalry Corps with 4,000 more cuirassiers and 2,000 men of the Imperial Guard's heavy cavalry. There was a pause while the new troops were deployed, during which the French artillery continued to pound Wellington's troops, then Ney once again led a charge.

This charge followed the same pattern as those before. The cavalry thundered up the slope to crest the ridge while taking casualties from artillery, then rode around the squares exchanging pistol shot for musket fire until both sides fell back on cold steel.

This time, with greater numbers and the men of the Imperial Guard, Ney achieved more. The British 15th Hussars were caught in open order by the Guard Dragoons and lost heavily, as did several units of Brunswick infantry.

When the Guard horse artillery joined the fray they poured fire into the densely packed men of the squares. An infantry division from d'Erlon's corps marched up the slope close to Hougoumont and deployed to open musket fire on the squares facing them. Both moves threatened to inflict massive casualties, but due to the restricted space they had in which to deploy neither could get fully into action. A charge by the 900 men of the Brunswick cavalry caused them to fall back.

At 6 pm Ney accepted that he could not batter his way through Wellington's army with cavalry and led his men back across the valley. He had been too busy with his cavalry charges and too deafened by the thundering roars of the grand battery to notice what had been going on elsewhere on the battlefield. When he got back to Napoleon's command post he must have been aghast at what he learned.

A new threat

It had been nearly six hours since Lobau's small corps had been sent to hold the right flank of Napoleon's army. Lobau had known that he was as likely to face a Prussian attack as to welcome Grouchy's forces, but for hours nothing had happened. He could hear the cannon and musketry coming from behind him as the attack on Wellington's ridge continued, but he received no word from his emperor. Once or twice Lobau had seen columns of men moving across open ground miles to the east, but they had been too far away to see if they were French or Prussian.

Lobau occupied his time deploying his men to block the roads coming from the east. He also sent units to secure the ground around the Smohain stream. The sun shone, the birds sang, time passed. Suddenly there was movement on the edge of a wood a mile to his south-east. Men were hauling two dozen cannon out of the trees and manhandling them into position.

Suddenly the cannon belched flames and smoke. Cannonballs began falling among Lobau's corps to kill and wound dozens of his men.

The Prussians had arrived.

CHAPTER 10

'AS IF BLOWN BY A WHIRLWIND'

**Marshal Grouchy describing the Prussian army in a
letter to Napoleon, 17 June 1815**

The Prussians, meanwhile, had been having problems of their
own. Before dawn a confidential message arrived from Müffling
giving Blücher his private view on Wellington's intentions and
abilities. He confirmed that Wellington had drawn up his army
to defend the ridge at Mont-Saint-Jean and that he intended to
fight. However, Müffling gave his opinion that Wellington
would not be able to hold out all day without Prussian help.

Blücher and Gneisenau discussed the situation. Gneisenau
in particular was still wary of Wellington's intentions, and both
men were painfully aware of the mauling their forces had
received at Ligny. For both reasons it was decided that the
Prussian advance to Waterloo would be led by the only corps
that had not been involved at Ligny and which was therefore
both fresh and at full strength: that of Bülow. The army's entire
baggage and supply train would go in the opposite direction,
to Louvain, in case a retreat to Germany proved necessary.

Slow progress

Bülow set out at dawn, at 7 am reaching Wavre – where the
bottleneck of the bridge over the river Dyle was expected to
cause delays. Entirely unexpected was the fact that a large house
in the high street caught fire just as Bülow's ammunition wagons
were trundling past. The potential for an explosion on an epic
scale was obvious. The march was abandoned and thousands
of men were thrown into the town to drag the wagons clear

and put out the fire. The affair delayed Bülow by more than two hours. It was 10 am before he marched out of Wavre.

At least one thing was not bothering the Prussians. Grouchy had delayed leaving Gembloux until he knew where the main Prussian army had gone to. As a consequence he was unlikely to reach Wavre until later in the afternoon.

Bülow's advance was at first speeded up by Gneisenau's decision to send the baggage train to Louvain. With no wagons in his column, Bülow could give priority to his cannon when it came to bridges or good roads, and hurry his infantry and cavalry forward over the open fields with speed. That speed soon slowed to a crawl.

The roads were entirely unsurfaced and after heavy rain had turned to mud. Pounded and stirred by thousands of hooves and booted feet, the mud fairly quickly turned into a quagmire of liquid goo that sucked at feet, pulled off boots and trapped horses while making the progress of artillery impossible. Time and again, pioneers had to come up to cut brushwood to lay over the mud so that artillery could pass. Elsewhere the fields gave way to dense woods, forcing the marching men either to return to the roads or take circuitous routes around the woods. It was all taking time, a great deal of time.

The occasional sighting of French light cavalry patrols caused even more delays. Bülow feared an ambush, and if caught strung out on the march he would have suffered a massacre. Time and again he had to halt his forward units in a defensive position to allow the rear units to catch up.

The defence of Wavre
Back at Wavre, things were still running less than smoothly. The III Corps of Thielmann had been ordered to be the last to leave Wavre. At about 3 pm Thielmann received reports from his scouts to the south that a large column of French soldiers was approaching. Grouchy had caught up with the Prussians. Having learned of the poor state of the roads he was expected

to take, Thielmann was just as worried about being caught in ambush as Bülow. He halted his men and put them into defensive positions around Wavre, at the same time sending messages to Blücher asking for orders.

The messenger arrived at 3.30 pm just as Blücher and Gneisenau had arrived on a hill near Lasne from which they could get a distant view of the Waterloo battlefield some kilometres to the west. They studied the scene through telescopes: they could see the smoke caused by artillery fire and the movement of larger masses of men. Although they did not know it, they were watching Wellington's reorganization after defeating d'Erlon's attack and Ney's assault on La Haye Sainte.

It was clear that a major battle was taking place, and that Wellington was managing to hold his own so far. Blücher wanted to steer Bülow's men directly west so that they would arrive on Wellington's left flank and give him support against Napoleon's assault. Gneisenau disagreed. He suggested sending Bülow south-west so that he would arrive behind Napoleon's right flank, cutting his line of retreat and falling on the rear of the French army. Such a plan would, if it succeeded, guarantee a total victory by crushing Napoleon. However, it ran the risk that Napoleon might manage to ambush the Prussians as they were on the march by falling on their exposed right flank.

After some discussion, Blücher and Gneisenau decided to direct Bülow south-west, while Zieten's I Corps would go west. This meant that the first Prussians on the scene would attack Napoleon's rear right flank, while those arriving later would go to the direct aid of Wellington.

Opposite: Marshal Blücher urges an artillery crew to hurry along the road to Waterloo on the morning of 18 June. The cross-country roads from Wavre to Waterloo were of poor quality and many had degenerated into mud after the heavy rains of the previous day.

Blücher sent off his orders, including instructions back to Wavre that Thielmann was to hold Wavre no matter what the cost in men. After the despatch riders had gone, Blücher turned to Gneisenau and said, 'It does not matter if Thielmann and all his men are killed, so long as they stop Grouchy from joining Napoleon.'

At Wavre, Thielmann was attacked at 4 pm. Thielmann had placed a strong advance guard south of the town in the hamlet of Aisemont. An attack of French infantry with artillery support soon drove the Prussians out of Aisemont and by about 4.30 pm the French had control of the south bank of the river Dyle.

Grouchy himself then came up and studied Thielmann's defences. He decided that Wavre was too strongly held to be taken without suffering heavy casualties. He kept some infantry in front of Wavre, together with some artillery to keep Thielmann's attention focused there, then sent infantry and cavalry to march to the flanks to try to find another way over the river.

At this crucial point Thielmann discovered that one of his four brigades had marched off to the west. The message he had sent to halt had gone astray, so General von Borcke had marched off with 7,000 of Thielmann's 22,000 men to go to Waterloo.

Grouchy, too, had received disturbing news. At 4 pm he received Napoleon's orders telling him to march to join the emperor before the Prussians arrived to support Wellington. By this time he was engaged against Thielmann and feared that if he pulled back, the Prussian would attack his outnumbered and retreating men. It would make more sense to make it look as if he intended to continue attacking Wavre.

Grouchy therefore allocated the task of continuing to mount attacks on Thielmann to Vandamme's III Corps of 16,000 men. Gérard's IV Corps of 15,000 men would meanwhile turn west and march through St Lambert to attack where he estimated the bulk of the Prussian army would be disorganized by marching along poor quality roads. It took him some time to get Gérard's men off the road north and turned west. Gérard had got only as far as Bierges when he was shot and badly wounded. His troops pushed on without him, however, but made slow progress.

Blücher plans attack

Meanwhile, Blücher had at 4 pm received a message from Müffling in which he gave a detailed account of the battle so far and how things looked from Wellington's ridge. Until this point, Blücher had been intending to await the arrival of Bülow's entire IV Corps before attacking.

The troops that had come up were hiding in a wood 1.5 km to the east of Plancenoit, facing the right flank of Lobau's corps. Having read Müffling's message, however, Blücher decided to attack at once. At 4.30 pm Bülow received orders to seize Plancenoit in order to outflank Lobau on the south, then to march straight on west for another 1.5 km to reach the main road south of Napoleon and cut off his line of retreat. Blücher was intending then to attack Lobau with Pirch's II Corps as soon as it arrived, while sending Zieten's I Corps to join up with Wellington.

It took a few minutes for Bülow to prepare his troops. Then he led his artillery out of the wood and opened fire with the salvo that surprised Lobau.

Gebhard Leberecht von Blücher

Blücher was born into an ancient but minor family of nobility in the small German state of Mecklenburg-Schwerin in 1742. As a younger son he took the traditional path of a military career, but since Mecklenburg-Schwerin had few opportunities to offer, he joined the Swedish army as an hussar. When Sweden went to war with Prussia, Blücher fought gallantly in Pomerania, but was captured. He found that the officer commanding the force that had captured him was a relative, Wilhelm von Belling. Invited to dinner, Blücher impressed von Belling who at once recruited him to serve as a Prussian staff officer. Blücher later fell out with King Frederick the Great and resigned from the army. He bought a farm and rapidly established himself as a successful businessman. After Frederick the Great's death, Blücher was offered command of the prestigious Seydlitz Hussars, famed for their red and silver uniforms. During the 1790s he gained fame as a cavalry commander in campaigns against Revolutionary France. After the Prussian defeat by Napoleon at Jena in 1806 he extricated some of the Prussian army before the rest surrendered and commanded a skilful fighting retreat to the Danish border. The Danes refused Blücher and his men sanctuary, so he was forced to surrender, a humiliation he never forgot nor forgave. Blücher became a national hero for his fighting retreat and agitated constantly for a renewed war with France. When war broke out in 1813, Blücher was given command of the Prussian army and fought tirelessly and ruthlessly against the French. Arriving in Paris after Napoleon's defeat in 1814 he ordered his men to blow up the Jena Bridge over the Seine, but after the first blast failed to demolish the bridge was stopped from further efforts by Wellington. After the Waterloo campaign he was increasingly troubled by the injuries he sustained at Ligny and retired to his country estate. He died in 1819.

CHAPTER 11

'UP, GUARDS, AND AT THEM AGAIN'

*Wellington's legendary (and disputed) exhortation to
the British Foot Guards*

The arrival of the Prussians completely changed the Battle of
Waterloo. Napoleon was no longer seeking to defeat Wellington
before turning on the Prussians the following day. He now
had to face both his enemies at once. Time was running out
for the French.

Lobau's first reaction to the arrival of the Prussians was to
send a messenger to Napoleon to announce the news. At the
same time he realized that there was a wide gap between the
Prussians' right flank and Wellington's left. Into this gap Lobau
pushed his cavalry, followed by infantry who barricaded themselves into the handful of houses overlooking the Smohain
stream. He also realized that the village of Plancenoit to the
south commanded the main Brussels road. He sent his infantry
reserves into the village.

As more and more Prussians emerged into sight, Lobau
reduced his frontage so as to increase the depth of his formations and concentrated around Plancenoit, leaving only a screen
to link his main force to Napoleon's right at the Smohain stream.
Lobau was confident he could hold his own against Bülow's
corps, but he had to assume that more Prussians were on the
way and that he might soon be in difficulties.

Attack on La Haye Sainte
Back on the main battlefield, Napoleon scanned Wellington's
ridge. He saw units being repositioned and correctly deduced

that Wellington was shifting regiments around to try to plug gaps. His eye fell on the farm of La Haye Sainte. If that fell to the French it would clear the way for a new assault on the weakest part of Wellington's centre. Napoleon sent Ney to take the farmhouse with those units of d'Erlon's corps that had reformed.

The Hanoverians in La Haye Sainte saw three divisions marching against them, preceded by a heavy artillery barrage that smashed holes in the walls. Baring's main problem, however, was a lack of ammunition. A man was sent running up the slope to Baring's senior, General Baron Ompteda. But after all the fighting on the ridge, Ompteda was short of ammunition himself. He sent off for ammunition from the rear, but for whatever reason it never arrived.

After an hour Baring's Hanoverians ran out of ammunition. They fell back on their bayonets, while some men threw stones and tiles down on the French from the roof. After attempting a last stand in the farmhouse, Baring and his surviving men retreated back up the slope to join Ompteda. Many of Baring's men were unfit for further duty due to wounds and were sent off to the medical teams working in the rear. Baring did a quick count. Of the 400 men he had had at dawn, only 42 now stood beside him.

The farmhouse had fallen. French artillery was brought up to fire at Wellington's centre at close range, while a final assault to smash its way to Brussels was drawn up.

Wellington redeploys his troops

These moves made it clear to Wellington that Napoleon was once again going to try to penetrate his centre. He had expected Napoleon to use his skills at manoeuvring, but this had not happened. Wellington decided to take the risk of weakening his flanks to strengthen his centre. The 3rd Dutch Division had been placed more than 1.5 km to the west to keep open Wellington's line of retreat. Those 6,000 men were now moved to the centre, as were the 2,000 light cavalry of Vivian and Vandeleur who had been out on the far left.

An immediate result of these changes came at the eastern end of the battlefield. Count Durutte, commanding the 4th Division of d'Erlon's corps, had not been heavily engaged so far – having acted as a flank guard during the great advance earlier. Now he saw the movement to the British centre and took the opportunity to attack Papelotte overlooking the dip of the Smohain stream. Sending forward infantry under cover of an artillery barrage, Durutte captured Papelotte without much difficulty and began barricading the buildings.

Further south, Lobau was holding his own. He was, however, losing men and watched with some alarm as more Prussians came marching out of the woods. These were the lead units of Pirch's II Corps, which meant that Lobau was now seriously outnumbered. He sent to Napoleon, announcing he could not hold Plancenoit much longer. Napoleon responded at 6.40 pm by sending to Plancenoit his Young Guard. This was the most junior division in the Imperial Guard, but it still contained 4,200 veterans. The arrival of the Young Guard stabilized the position and pushed the Prussians back.

At La Haye Sainte, the advanced French artillery and infantry were having a devastating effect on the centre of Wellington's position. Ney had brought up several regiments of heavy cavalry, who forced the defenders to form square. Into these dense formations the French gunners were pouring a torrent of fire. The Inniskillings were down to 218 men, having started the day with 700 while the 1st Nassau Regiment had lost 70 per cent of itsmen while the 5th Netherlanders had lost more than 90 per cent of its men and its colours. The surviving officers of the British 30th Foot were so worried that they cut their regimental colours

Opposite: The French attack on La Haye Sainte in the early evening. The farmhouse is on the left, the sandpit on the right. The outbuildings are wreathed in smoke and barely visible. Wellington's position on the hill behind has been brought forward by the artist; in reality he was several hundred yards away.

from their poles, handed them to a sergeant and told him to head to the rear, find a horse and be ready to flee to the safety of the Royal Navy.

Ney, watching these events unfold, decided that the time had come to crush Wellington. He sent a message to Napoleon requesting extra men with which to win the battle. Ney's message arrived just after Napoleon learned that his Young Guard had been pushed out of Plancenoit by new Prussian reinforcements. Prussian artillery were beginning to send occasional balls over the main road, threatening Napoleon's line of retreat.

Napoleon snapped back at Ney's messenger, 'Men? Where does he expect me to get them? Does he think I can make them?'

Old Guard retake Plancenoit

Instead, Napoleon ordered two battalions of his Old Guard – the elite of the elite – to recapture Plancenoit. Napoleon ordered that his Guard should not fire their muskets but must use their bayonets. He fully understood the morale effect that these older veterans in their towering bearskins hats and elaborate uniforms would have on the Prussians. The Old Guard was composed only of men over the age of 35 who had 10 years' experience and had fought in at least three battles. They were trained in advanced fighting techniques and given the very finest equipment. Moreover, the Guard battalions each had 200 more men than a normal battalion.

The Old Guard did not disappoint. They deployed into line and marched on Plancenoit with their drums beating. After some desultory resistance, the Prussians turned and fled. In all 14 Prussian battalions fled in front of two from the Old Guard, tumbling back in confusion. Spurred on by this success, the

Opposite: The Prince of Orange is wounded while a British dragoon carries a captured French standard past him. Despite the heroic stance of the prince in this picture, the impact of the bullet in his left shoulder actually threw him from his horse and dumped him on his back in the mud.

Young Guard charged forward and completed the rout of the Prussians. Bülow and Pirch were back where they had started.

With his right flank and line of retreat now secure, Napoleon could pay attention to Wellington again. At about 7.15 pm Napoleon received two messages. The first came from Lobau. He had seen columns of men to the south-east and identified them as being Grouchy's French. With Grouchy attacking Blücher's rear the Prussians would be unable to interfere any further. The second was brought by Ney himself who emphasized the shattered state of Wellington's centre.

Fresh French assault

Newly galvanized, Napoleon threw himself into the final destruction of Wellington's army. He allocated Ney five battalions of the Old and Middle Guard, with orders to attack in column up the slope to the left of La Haye Sainte, where the defences were seen to be weakest. Accompanying them were the horse artillery of the Guard. Napoleon sent orders to Reille that he was to send any of his men not committed at Hougoumont to act as a flank guard on the Guard's left. D'Erlon was to attack up the slope to the right of La Haye Sainte. Heavy cavalry were to bring up the rear, ready to charge forward to exploit the gap that was going to be opened up by the Guard infantry.

The grand battery again roared out its hail of balls and shells to deluge the survivors on Wellington's ridge with a new onslaught of death. Under cover of the cannon fire, the Guard advanced with drums beating and flags waving. On battlefields across Europe the advance of the Guard had heralded inevitable victory. Enemies had fled at the mere sight of the bearskins on the march. Morale in the French army soared and there was a general movement forward.

Opposite: By the evening of 18 June, Napoleon's situation was critical. Grouchy had not arrived, while the Prussians were pressuring his right flank. Only the Guard breaking through Wellington's centre could help.

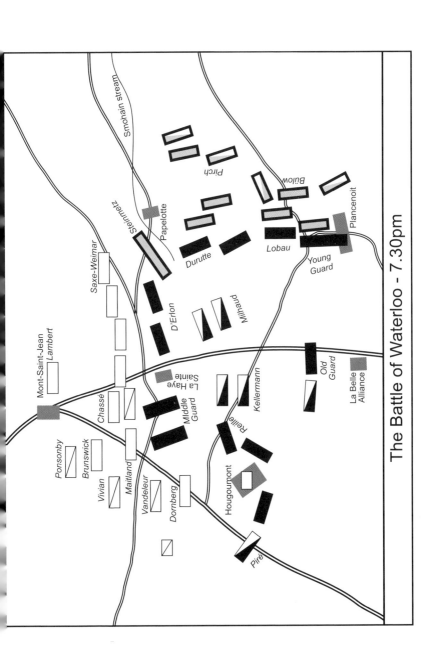

The Battle of Waterloo - 7.30pm

Wellington, however, had not been idle. He had seen the smoke over Plancenoit and guessed it meant that Blücher was arriving. Leaving only a few Dutch troops to watch the French at Papelotte, Wellington abandoned his left and drew those troops to his centre. The Brunswickers were similarly moved from the right to the centre.

Senior commanders were not immune: the Prince of Orange was hurt, de Lancey was mortally wounded and Wellington's staff was reduced to just a single officer – Captain Shaw.

As the five battalions of the Middle Guard marched forward, Napoleon rode up to salute them as they passed. The three battalions of the Old Guard stayed beside their emperor to act as a mobile reserve while Ney rode at the head of the attacking columns.

Ney divided his force into two. The 1/3rd and 4th Grenadiers went straight up the hill just west of La Haye Sainte, while the 2/3rd Chasseurs and both battalions of the 4th Chasseurs inclined slightly to the west so that a gap opened up between the two columns. Halfway up the slope, Ney's horse was shot dead so the marshal continued on foot.

The first column reached the crest of the ridge where they met what was left of the British 30th, 33rd, 69th and 73rd infantry regiments. Those redcoats were being pushed back when out of the smoke there came galloping the horse artillery of Chassé's Dutch 3rd Division. They unlimbered and poured into the 1/3rd Grenadiers a salvo of deadly canister shot at almost point blank range. More than 100 French went down in that first blast, and more when the second salvo was fired.

British and Dutch resistance

Hidden behind the artillery smoke the 6,000 infantry of the Dutch 3rd Division had formed up in several dense columns, then fixed bayonets. Now they came storming out of the smoke, screaming defiance and plunged into the decimated ranks of the 1/3rd

Grenadiers – and caught the 4th Grenadiers as they were deploying to meet them. The 1/3rd Grenadiers fell back in disorder, while the 4th Grenadiers also fell back but in good order, managing to hold the Dutch off.

Meanwhile the other column of the Guard had also crested the ridge. The 2/3rd Chasseurs came up first and saw ahead of them nothing but empty fields with some cavalry wheeling in the distance. Wellington, who was nearby on his horse, urged his men to action, at which the British Foot Guards sprang to their feet and poured a devastating volley into the Chasseurs. The guards had been lying down among the standing rye to try to avoid the French cannon fire. Their sudden appearance, as much as their musketry, halted the French.

Seeing the French hesitate, the British Guards cheered, then charged with their bayonets. The 2/3rd Chasseurs fell back in some disorder, with the British Guards after them. As the two battalions of the 4th Chasseurs came up the British Guards fell back in disorder, their light companies skirmishing in an effort to cover their withdrawal. The 4th Chasseurs now crested the ridge, firing a volley to cut down the Dutch gunners who had done so much damage to the Grenadiers, while firing steadily at the retreating British Guards.

At this point John Colborne – in command of the British 52nd Light Infantry, to the right of the British Guards – realized that there were no French units in front of his men. Without orders he marched his regiment down the slope then wheeled to the left to bring his men in line facing the left flank of the 4th Chasseurs. It was now that the professional training of the British infantry proved crucial. Able to fire four volleys a minute, compared to the two or three of other armies, the British could put down a massive volume of fire. Colborne now poured this awesome fire into the flank of the Chasseurs.

Recognizing a crucial moment when he saw one, Wellington spurred over. 'Go on, Colborne,' he shouted. 'They won't stand.'

Colborne's men fixed bayonets and charged as a regiment

of Hanoverians came up on their right to threaten the rear of the Chasseurs. With that, the Chasseurs turned and retreated, pursued down the slope by Colborne, the Hanoverians and the British Guards.

The Prussians confer

Meanwhile, Müffling had been called to the extreme left flank beyond Papelotte, where the Dutch 28th Foot was in difficulties. This regiment was still dressed in the blue jackets and wide-topped shakos they had worn when in French service. Some Prussian artillery had, perhaps understandably, thought that they were French – and opened fire. Müffling went galloping over to order the Prussians to cease fire.

Having restored order, Müffling met Reiche, Chief of Staff to Zeiten and the Prussian I Corps. Müffling explained the dire situation in Wellington's centre with the Imperial Guard advancing, and urged Reiche to march directly west to reinforce Wellington. Reiche promised to do so, at which Müffling rode off to report to Wellington. Reiche sent an order to General Steinmetz, who commanded the lead units of I Corps, to halt until the rest of the corps came up and then himself went to find Zieten who was in the rear hurrying his slower units.

The unfortunate Reiche had ridden only three-quarters of a kilometre when one of Blücher's personal staff officers galloped up from Plancenoit. This officer told Reiche that the I Corps had to turn south to help Blücher who was under attack from Napoleon's Guard. As the two men talked, Steinmetz galloped up in angry mood. He demanded to know why he had been ordered to halt just as he was about to attack the French. A furious row between the three men then ensued. It ended when Steinmetz demanded to know if either man had specific orders addressed to him in person from either Blücher or Zeiten. Neither man had.

Steinmetz leads flank attack

'Right', declared Steinmetz. 'Then I am going to attack the French that I can see in front of me. You two can do what you like.' With that, he galloped back to his men and gave the order to advance. He led them along the banks of the Smohain stream so that they would be out of the line of fire of the cannon ahead of them. Fortuitously, this also meant that they were out of sight of the French as well. When Steinmetz's column marched up out of the Smohain dip they found themselves on the flank of the reeling French attack on Wellington's ridge. There could be no mistaking the Prussian flags, which were over 1.75 m square, boldly patterned in black and white and dominated by a great black eagle. The unexpected sight of dense columns of Prussian infantry appearing out of the hidden valley just as the Imperial Guard was falling back was too much for the battered French.

The men of d'Erlon's corps turned and ran, all formation and cohesion utterly lost. The panic spread rapidly as the shouts of 'The Guard retreats!' mingled with those of 'The Prussians are here!' Within just ten minutes the French army collapsed into a fleeing mob.

CHAPTER 12

'MERDE'

Word shouted by members of Napoleon's Old Guard when called upon to surrender towards the end of the battle

Seeing the French army collapse into confusion and rout, Wellington spurred his horse to the top of the ridge where he could be seen more easily. He then stood up in his stirrups and waved his hat forwards three times to indicate that he wanted the entire army to chase the French.

Many units formed up and began to advance, but others did not. Several infantry regiments that had been fighting all day simply sat down where they were. The heavy cavalry had been badly battered, and had charged again and again to drive the French cavalry off the defensive squares in the afternoon. They, too, failed to move. The fresher light cavalry of Vivian and Vandeleur, however, spurred forward to disrupt any efforts by the French to re-form or stand.

The French take flight

Amidst the chaos, Ney was on foot. He sought to rally retreating infantry by shouting at them, 'Come and see how a marshal of France dies!' He managed to put together a small force, but then

Opposite: The confusion of the closing stages of the battle are shown here. British hussars wearing shakos hack their way through the lancers of Napoleon's Guard while British infantry bayonet French Guardsmen. In the background more British cavalry push forward while the French army fragments.

an officer rode up and shouted, 'The Prussians are here,' where-upon they all fled again.

Napoleon watched the rapidly unfolding disaster with dismay. He stationed the four battalions of the Old Guard drawn up in square to block the main road, supported by four squadrons of Guard cavalry. He took refuge in one of the squares for a while. Then he mounted a horse and, taking one squadron of light Guard cavalry with him, rode off to the south. His last orders were that the Guard was to slow down the British advance while he rallied the fleeing army and linked up with Grouchy. Then he was off.

Soon afterwards, Ney arrived at the four squares and took refuge in them. A Major Rullière put him on a horse and told him to find Napoleon. The dazed Ney did not seem to hear him properly. He was still gripping in his hand the hilt of his broken sword. Rullière shouted again, this time Ney nodded and spurred away.

Wellington was watching the pursuit develop from his horse on the top of the ridge. Beside him sat the Earl of Uxbridge. One of the last cannonballs fired by the French that day struck the ground in front of them, splattering both men with mud. Feeling something strike him, Uxbridge looked down to see that the ball had bounced up and smashed his right leg to a bloody pulp.

'Good God, Sir', he gasped. 'I've lost my leg.'

Wellington turned and after a quick glance replied, 'Good God, Sir. So you have,' before summoning men to carry the stricken earl to the temporary hospital behind the army.

Old Guard in retreat

The four squares of the Old Guard were now facing the advancing British army. The British were almost as disorganized as the fleeing mob of Frenchmen that they were chasing. The squares drove off disorganized assaults by

British infantry, though musketry caused casualties. Attacks by the light cavalry of Vandeleur were more serious, but when the three squadrons of Guard cavalry showed themselves, Vandeleur pulled his men away to go after easier prey.

The Guard now began to march south along the main road, stopping every now and then to fire at their pursuers or redress their lines. By 9 pm they were the only organized French units left standing. Artillery fire reduced their numbers dramatically, but still they retreated in good order.

When the squares reached La Belle Alliance they were approached by Lord Hill, commander of Wellington's II Corps. He called on them to surrender, politely doffing his hat as he did so. The response is disputed, but it seems that an officer shouted back, 'The Guard dies, it does not surrender.' Others called out simply the swear word *merde*. Hill then opened fire with artillery and sent in his light cavalry to complete the slaughter.

Amazingly the square of the 2/3rd Grenadiers managed to escape and as darkness gathered it retreated further down the main road. It finally broke up around 11 pm and the men joined the fleeing mob.

Soon after dark, Blücher and Wellington met at *La Belle Alliance*. Wellington said that his army was too battered to pursue the French, so the chase was taken up by the Prussians.

Blücher gave orders that no mercy was to be shown to the French, and his men enthusiastically put the orders into practice. Wounded men were killed where they lay, no prisoners were taken and any Frenchman who could not run fast enough was killed.

At Genappe the Prussians ran into a barricade of wagons and other debris manned by French firing muskets. There was a delay while the Prussians brought up artillery to blast the obstacle apart, then the chase went on.

THE DUKE OF WELLINGTON

Arthur Wellesley was born in Dublin in 1769 into a wealthy Anglo-Irish family. He joined the British army at the age of 19, being famously dismissed by his own mother with the words, 'Poor Arthur is fit for nothing but cannon fodder.' Despite this, his family used their connections to get him appointed aide to the lord lieutenant of Ireland, where his talents and capacity for hard work were noticed. This, together with family connections, ensured his early rapid rise through the ranks to the rank of colonel by 1796. He then went to India, where he won a series of battles and campaigns – most notably, Assaye in 1803. He returned to Britain as a lieutenant general and was fortunate to be available when General John Moore was killed at Corunna, necessitating an urgent replacement to take over command of British forces in the Spanish Peninsula. Wellesley arrived in Portugal in 1808 and within days had defeated the local French forces at Roliça. The following years brought a series of victories, with very few minor setbacks, which ensured Wellesley's increasing prestige, fame and the bestowal on him of a hat-trick of dukedoms in Portugal, Spain and Britain by 1814. After the Battle of Waterloo, the Duke of Wellington (as he now was) went into politics and became a government minister in 1818. By 1828 he was prime minister, during which his most famous act was the Catholic Emancipation Act that gave full rights to Roman Catholics in Ireland. He stood down as prime minister in 1830 and retired from public life in 1846. He died in 1852 and was given a lavish state funeral that took him to his impressive tomb in St Paul's Cathedral, London.

Just beyond the barricade the Prussians found Napoleon's hastily abandoned carriage. Inside were found the emperor's hat, sword, writing book and a pouch containing a bag of top-quality diamonds. Clearly Napoleon had left only minutes earlier. Try as they might, the vengeful Prussians could not find him. If they had, they would undoubtedly have killed him.

Wellington's despatch

After talking to Blücher, Wellington returned to his quarters in Waterloo. He could not go to bed as that was occupied by his aide Colonel Gordon, dying slowly of his wounds. Although exhausted, Wellington sat down to write his official despatch to London. The document ran to more than 2,300 words. Wellington handed it to Major Henry Percy, the only aide-de-camp who was still with him, to carry to London.

Percy had, in fact, been shot in the foot and had been hiding the wound from Wellington. He rode as far as Brussels before hiring a fast carriage to take him on. After crossing the Channel, Percy hired another carriage to take him to London. He arrived at 10 pm on 21 June and hurried to deliver the letter to Lord Bathurst, Minister for War. Bathurst was not in his office, but having supper in Grosvenor Square. Bathurst did not bother to read the letter, but as soon as Percy announced that Napoleon was defeated he bundled the young man into a coach and hurried to St James's Square where the Prince Regent was attending a ball.

Percy arrived at the ball in the same clothes that he had been wearing at the Duchess of Richmond's ball. He had not had time to change in the intervening six days, and was caked in mud and blood as he limped in. The room fell silent as the bloodied young man staggered in carrying two captured French eagles. Recognizing the prince, Percy fell to one knee and handed over the eagles.

The Prince Regent was jubilant and invited Percy to join an impromptu celebration. It was soon clear, however, that Percy was utterly exhausted. Instead, the Prince Regent sent Percy to his father's house, where he collapsed into bed and slept for 18 hours.

CHAPTER 13

'TO THROW MYSELF UPON THE HOSPITALITY OF YOUR PRINCE'

Words spoken by Napoleon on surrendering to Captain Maitland of HMS Bellerophon

Fleeing south from Waterloo, Napoleon at first hoped to rally some of his men the next day, then link up with Grouchy. It was quickly obvious that none of the soldiers was likely to reform. The ruthless brutality of the Prussians meant that all anyone wanted to do was run away. Nor was Grouchy going to be any use. He was far to the north-east at Wavre and would take some time to rejoin Napoleon.

Instead, Napoleon rode to Paris as quickly as he could. He knew that France had somewhere between 200,000 and 300,000 men under arms and hoped that he would be able to get a new army into the field before the allies reached Paris. He sent Soult to find Grouchy and order him to fight a rearguard campaign to slow Wellington and Blücher. This Grouchy did with rather more skill than he had displayed when chasing the Prussians, but to no avail.

Napoleon reached Paris on 21 June to find that the National Assembly and government had turned against him. He had promised them a quick and spectacular victory that would disrupt the enemy alliance and ensure peace for France. He had failed to deliver, and nobody in Paris had the taste for a long, drawn-out war. After several days of tense negotiations, Napoleon admitted defeat. He abdicated as emperor on 22 June and three days later vanished from Paris in a carriage with a small escort.

Austrian and German movements

While the Waterloo campaign was unfolding, Engelhardt and his German corps had reached their first objective of Arlon in the southern Netherlands. He then pushed cavalry patrols out to the west and north to try to locate the armies of Napoleon, Wellington and Blücher, which he knew to be in the Netherlands, but did not know where. On 21 June a message came from Blücher announcing the victory at Waterloo and urging Engelhardt to advance into France as planned. The next day the Germans were on the move to lay siege to the fortresses of Sedan, Bouillon, Montmédy, Laon and Rheims. Sedan fell quickly, surrendering on 25 June, but the other two places held out.

Meanwhile, the Austrian commander Prince Schwarzenberg was waiting on the Rhine with a large army of Austrians and Germans. He had been ordered to await the arrival of the vast Russian army of Tolly before commencing his advance in the first week of July. However, on 17 June, he heard that Napoleon had entered the Netherlands two days earlier. Schwarzenberg at once disproved his reputation for caution by ordering an immediate invasion of France by whichever troops were ready to do so. His aim was to defeat the French forces facing him – which he knew must be a fairly small force if the main French army was with Napoleon – and to cause as much trouble as possible in the hope of causing Napoleon to detach forces from his main army and so relieve the pressure on Wellington and Blücher.

On 19 June, the day after the Battle of Waterloo but before news of that battle reached the Rhine, the Bavarian army crossed the Rhine on barges, then marched west towards the Sarre river. Four days later, after some minor skirmishing, the Bavarians secured bridges over the Sarre at Saarbrücken and Sarreguemines. More severe fighting took place on 24 June as the Bavarians moved toward Luneville, and when they reached the fortress of Bitche they found a strong garrison under Brigadier-General Creutzer, who refused to surrender.

Meanwhile a column of Austrians, with some forces of the

Russian advance guard, was marching towards Nancy. They reached that city on 28 June and made it their headquarters. Forces were sent out toward Metz and Chalons-sur-Marne. The Russians in Schwarzenberg's army set about systematically plundering the entire area, causing him a good deal of trouble as he was seeking to keep the French civilians content in the hope that they would turn against Napoleon. The Austrian advance ground to a halt.

Württemberg engages Rapp

The rest of the large Austrian army had meanwhile been getting moving and was advancing on a broad front from the Rhine. On 28 June, the III Corps under the command of Crown Prince Wilhelm of Württemberg reached La Suffel (now Souffelweyersheim), where they found the French V Corps under Marshal Jean Rapp blocking their path. Württemberg quickly realized that with his 40,000 men he outnumbered Rapp by more than two to one, and launched an attack.

The Austrian attack pushed the French back across the open ground, though the French did not lose cohesion as they retreated. Rapp, standing with his reserves on the nearby hill of Niederhausbergen, noticed that the Austrian left flank was becoming exposed as it advanced. Ordering his reserve infantry to follow on as quickly as possible in column, Rapp led two regiments of cavalry down the hill and charged headlong in to the Austrian flank. The crashing impact of the French cavalry threw the Austrians into confusion. When the French infantry came up and opened fire, the Austrians collapsed and fled. The panic spread along the line and soon the entire Austrian army was in retreat.

Opposite: The scene at Waterloo the day after the battle. The speed of Wellington's pursuit of Napoleon meant that the dead and wounded remained in the open longer than was normal. Families and comrades searched for the missing, hoping to carry them to the field hospitals set up behind the lines.

BATTLE OF WATERLOO.

W. Scott's Poem, Pᵗ 96.

Published by E. Gould, April 22 1818 by Edw. Orme, Publisher to his Majesty & H.R.H. the Prince Regent, Bond Street, corner of New Bond Street, London.

J.M. Clark del.t   M. Dubourg sculpt

So rapid was the Austrian collapse that Rapp's cavalry were able to capture Württemberg's carriage, paperwork and most of his supplies and baggage. The pursuit went on for more than 15 km, but came to a sudden halt when large numbers of soldiers were spotted in the distance. This was a force of 30,000 Russians hurrying forward to the sound of guns. Rapp halted the pursuit, and marched back to his start lines to prepare a rearguard action. The Russians then proceeded to loot every village within reach and set fire to the houses and churches.

Appalled by the behaviour of the Russians, and aware of the advance of Wellington and Blücher, Rapp sent a messenger to Württemberg, suggesting an armistice. He asked for time to send a messenger to Paris for orders, and that the Russians be withdrawn until an answer was received. Württemberg, smarting from this defeat, refused.

Knowing from his scouts that some 70,000 Austrians and Russians were advancing against him, Rapp fell back to the fortified city of Strasbourg and prepared to endure a long siege. Before entering Strasbourg, Rapp put garrisons into Strasbourg, Landau, La Petite-Pierre, Huningue, Sélestat, Lichtenberg, Phalsbourg, Neuf-Brisach and Belfort with orders to hold out for as long as possible.

Frimont's attack from the south

Further south, the Austro-Italian army under Frimont had been advancing into southern France from Italy. On 21 June Frimont had his first clash with the French of Marshal Suchet's Army of the Alps at the Pass of Meillerie. Suchet had started his own advance on 14 June, the same day as Frimont. He had reached Geneva next day, and left behind a small force to conduct a siege while marching on to grab the passes at Meillerie and St Maurice.

Suchet reached the passes first, but had not yet finished fortifying the positions when the larger army of Frimont arrived. After a short, stiff fight Suchet fell back and by 27 June was back on the river Arve inside France. Frimont's left-hand column, meanwhile, had met little opposition and got over the Mount Cenis Pass without difficulty. On 28 June the column reached the town of Conflans (now Albertville) where it met a force sent by Suchet to block its advance. After a stiff fight, the Austrians got control of Conflans, but could not advance any further.

The right-hand column, meanwhile, had crossed the Arve and relieved Geneva. They were stopped on 29 June at the Pass of Les Rousses by strongly defended French redoubts and the campaign paused.

Lamarque takes on royalists in the Vendée

Another area in which the fighting was very far from over was the Vendée. Royalist noblemen Suzannet and Autichamp had been on the defensive since Napoleon had arrived in Paris. The Napoleonic commander, General Lamarque, had spent the intervening weeks building up his strength. On 17 June, he finally felt strong enough to move with his 7,000 men to face the royalists' 9,000.

On 20 June, Lamarque attacked the royalists at Rocheservière. After some preliminary cavalry skirmishing, Suzannet led an infantry attack across open heathland. When Suzannet was hit by a bullet and collapsed, mortally wounded, his men fled. Autichamp managed to organize a fighting retreat with a small rearguard and so saved the royalists from total defeat.

Autichamp retreated back to Cholet, where he adopted a strong defensive position that he thought he could hold for some weeks. On 25 June, news arrived that Napoleon had defeated the Prussians at Ligny. That prompted Autichamp to accept a truce under which he retained the town of Cholet but undertook to launch no offensive actions in return for a cease-fire. On 29 June, news of Waterloo arrived, prompting Autichamp and Lamarque to meet again. This time the terms of the truce were confirmed almost unaltered and both sides sat down to await developments.

The developments turned out to be the arrival of some Prussian cavalry, to whom Lamarque surrendered his men before fleeing into exile. He returned to France on being pardoned in 1819 and spent the next decade or so devoted to the cause of agricultural improvements and social reform. Lamarque died in Paris in 1832. His funeral on 5 June attracted a vast crowd, which turned into a general protest against the government of King Louis Philippe. The protest escalated into a riot, which in turn became the 'June Rebellion' in which more than 800 people died. The funeral and subsequent uprising were immortalized in the Victor Hugo novel *Les Misérables*, and the subsequent stage and movie versions.

Autichamp resumed his pre-war government positions and faded into gentle obscurity.

Austrians and Russians on the move

On 4 July Schwarzenberg received an urgent message from Blücher asking him to march on Paris as quickly as possible. Schwarzenberg again chose the Bavarians to lead the advance and on 7 July the advance cavalry scouts of the Bavarians linked up with some Prussian cavalry units at Epernay. Blücher sent word asking the Bavarians to veer to the south, blocking the Marne Valley.

Hearing of the outbreak of hostilities, Tolly had ordered his columns of Russian troops to speed up across Germany. The lead units reached the Rhine about 24 June and went across the river to follow the Austrians the following day. The Russian army was thrown forward piecemeal as it arrived and lost its cohesion as an army. Instead, the various divisions were assigned to Austrian columns as they came up, so Tolly found that he had little to do except to co-ordinate the movements of his more slowly moving units and seek to sort out the customary confused state of his supply system.

Frimont and Suchet

Meanwhile, Frimont resumed his attacks on the passes over the Jura Mountains on 4 July. This time he succeeded by weight of numbers in pushing Suchet back. Suchet fought a skilled retreat, blowing up bridges and blasting holes in roads to slow the Austro-Italian supply wagons.

Once Frimont was out of the mountains, his advance was rapid. On 12 July, he reached the great city of Lyons, where Suchet and his army were waiting. Envoys from Suchet rode forwards seeking an armistice. Frimont and Suchet agreed that fighting on their front would come to an immediate end. Suchet agreed to evacuate his forces to the west banks of the Rhône and Saône rivers, handing over the cities of Lyons, Mâcon and Valence to the Austro-Italians. The rival armies would then go into camp and await news from the main theatre of war in the north. Frimont then sent a force north up the Saône to ensure that the French forces had evacuated the east bank as agreed.

While Frimont had been fighting his way over the mountains, an army of Piedmontese-Sardinian troops commanded by Lieutenant General d'Osasco had been working along the coast. They captured Nice on 9 July, and pushed forward meeting minimal resistance from the French Armée du Var under Marshal Brune. When news of the armistice between Frimont and Suchet arrived, d'Osasco and Brune likewise called a cease-fire.

With Rapp bottled up in Strasbourg, Schwarzenberg decided he could risk spreading his units out to cover and occupy as much of eastern France as possible. On 20 July, forward cavalry units reached Autun, where they met units of Frimont's army pushing north up the Saône to ensure that Suchet had, as he had promised, pulled his troops back to the west bank of that river.

Napoleon surrenders

Five days before Schwarzenberg's forces met those of Frimont at Autun the Royal Navy warship HMS *Bellerophon* had been patrolling off the French Atlantic port of La Rochelle. Captain Frederick Maitland saw his ship being approached by a small French smack. On board was the famous cartographer and author Count de Las Casas, who announced that he was the emissary of Napoleon and asked Maitland to talk.

Casas told Maitland that Napoleon had been offered political asylum in the United States of America, and asked that the ship carrying the former emperor be allowed to pass. Maitland had orders to allow no French craft to leave port and was uncertain what to do about this sudden diplomatic conundrum. He told Casas that he was prepared to take Napoleon on board and sail to Britain to see what the British government decided.

Casas left and returned with Napoleon. The former emperor climbed aboard and approached Maitland. He then lifted his hat, bowed and announced, 'I am come to throw myself on the hospitality of your prince and your laws.' Maitland moved out of his own cabin, which was given to Napoleon, while other ship's officers made space for Napoleon's retinue.

As it transpired, the British government was not entirely certain what to do with Napoleon. In the end, he was sent to live in exile, under armed guard, on the remote island of St Helena in the South Atlantic for the rest of his life.

Aftermath of the war

News reached Rapp in Strasbourg of Napoleon's submission and the end of hostilities in early August, but he still refused to surrender. Although the war was clearly over, for the men

Opposite: Napoleon arrives on board HMS *Bellerophon* on 15 July 1815. Napoleon was treated with all the dignities due to his imperial status. Captain Maitland vacated his own cabin for him.

bottled up in fortresses the length and breadth of France the future was not entirely clear. For a start, these garrisons were genuinely isolated in a way that modern soldiers would find hard to understand. With no radios or telephones, the garrisons were reliant on their surrounding enemy for news of the outside world. Just because an Austrian general said the war was over did not mean that it was. The message might simply be a trick to get the garrison to surrender.

Perhaps more pressing was the issue of retribution. Those soldiers who had taken up arms for Napoleon had quite clearly taken up arms against King Louis XVIII. Many soldiers and officers had sworn an oath of loyalty to Louis in 1814, which made them traitors. It was not entirely certain how forgiving Louis was likely to be of such treachery. Given the track record of the returning noble émigrés in 1814, it did not seem likely that Louis would be prepared to overlook the crime. Imprisonment or execution seemed likely punishments. The soldiers in garrisons knew that they were safe where they were, at least for the time being, and were understandably reluctant to give up their arms until they knew exactly where they stood with regard to King Louis.

They had good reason to be wary. De la Bédoyère had been arrested, court-martialled and shot in August. Ney was under arrest for treason, and would be executed in December. Murat was also under arrest, and would be shot by firing squad in October. Others would suffer a similar fate.

It was not until early September that a French general approached the walls of Strasbourg under the flag of the King of France. He brought with him a proclamation which, after he had read it himself, Rapp had read out to the troops. King Louis of France offered to pay all the soldiers their back pay immediately in cash, together with a bonus. On payment of the money, the regiments were to be disbanded and the men allowed to go home without any interference from the Austrians. The war, the king said, was over.

Rapp told his men to think over the offer, then report to their officers who in turn would report to him. The men decided to accept the offer. They laid down their weapons and marched out of Strasbourg under the eyes of the watching Austrians. As promised, the men were paid and then allowed to wander off as they wished. Rapp himself was not certain if the terms extended to himself. He went to Switzerland and wrote a letter to King Louis asking permission to live at his home in France. Permission was granted and he went home to Colmar in October 1815.

The German Corps had meanwhile been sitting in front of the fortresses in north-eastern France that they had been tasked with capturing. After Sedan fell on 25 June they had hoped for quick success, but by the end of July only Rheims had been captured. Even then, Engelhardt had agreed to terms under which the French garrison left with its arms and equipment intact, promising only to retreat to the Loire Valley. It was not until 20 September that the final fortress, Montmédy, capitulated. Again the terms were generous, with the French defenders being allowed to leave unmolested.

The war was finally over.

Index

Picture Credits

Corbis: 25 (Leemage), 51 (Leemage), 89 (Stapleton Collection), 93 (The Print Collector), 103 (Christie's Images), 123 (Burstein Collection), 129, 139 (Don Troiani), 147 (Bettmann), 155 (Heritage Images), 175 (Don Troiani)

Getty Images: 55 (Culture Club), 73 (Kean Collection), 83 (Kean Collection)

Mary Evans Picture Library: 63 (The National Army Museum)

Shutterstock: 9 (Georgios Kollidas), 21 (Morphart Creation), 33 (BVA), 67 (Morphart Creation), 111 (Georgios Kollidas), 151 (Nicku), 169 (Georgios Kollidas), 181 (Morphart Creation)

Topfoto: 96 (Roger-Viollet)

Maps: 45, 59, 159 © Rupert Matthews